Copyright © 2022 Zoe Lambreas

All images belong to the author, are out of copyright or are used by permission.

Editing: Zoe Lambreas

Typographic Design: Zoe Lambreas

All rights reserved. No part of this publication may be reproduced, stored in a retrieval system, or transmitted in any form or by any means-for example, electronic, photocopy, recording-without the prior written permission of the author. The only exception is brief quotations in printed reviews.

ISBN:978-0-9946333-0-9

First printing: January 2022, Melbourne by ZR Enterprises edited & reprinted: Aug. & Dec 2023; May, July 2024

SELA Books
www.speaklikeaustralians.com

The cover photograph shows Theo and Argyro with baby Voula. Behind them is a country-side view of sheep in Hamilton, in Victoria.

Speak English like Australians!

(True Stories of Australian Kids with Migrant Parents)

Zoe Lambreas

Listen to these stories on the Internet. Search for my name, Zoe Lambreas to find my website: www.speaklikeaustralians.com Then click the AUDIOS tab on the top. Or scan this code with your mobile QR scanner:

Or you can go to YouTube and search for Zoe Lambreas-Chapter 1 for example. There are other videos on YouTube as well like the alphabet, the Aussie sounds and more.

If you like to practise more English, there are four Speak English Like Australians! EAL/EFL Grammar & Activities Textbooks to use with this book of stories. There are answers for all the exercises in the books too. For more information please go to the above website.

Acknowledgment

I would like to thank each one of my dear family who were very kind and recorded the stories in this book for my website. I will never forget your help. Because of you, people can listen to the stories to improve their pronunciation, by searching for my name, Zoe Lambreas or scanning this QR code.

A special thank you to my wonderful husband for his help and encouragement over the years.

Thank you also to my friends at work for their help and ideas, as well as their recordings of stories.

Dedication

This book is for my much loved parents, Argyro and Theo Lambreas, who were very brave to move to Australia because they wanted a better life for their children. They worked hard and helped Australia to grow too. Because of all their hard work, Australia has become "the land of plenty" and God has blessed their family.

Of course, this book is also dedicated to my amazing brothers, Peter and Jim, who gave me so many memories from our childhood.

Zoe Lambreas

Foreword

I feel excited to introduce *Speak English like Australians – True Adventures of Aussie Kids with Migrant Parents*, which is a delightful set of simplified stories from the novel *A Walk in my Skin* by Zoe Lambreas, suited to literacy learners and those with dyslexia. You can almost hear the authentic voices of the family as she regales readers with their stories. Beginning from *Chapter 1 Coming to Australia*, when the main character, Theo, moves from Greece to Australia ("How you going Mike?") and *Chapter 2 Becoming an Aussie* ("Australia sure was a strange place!") to *The Marriage Proposal* (via letter and photo!), to eventually *Chapter 32 New Places* when Voula's family moves to Melbourne from the country town of Hamilton. There are 32 stories in all, which are written in such fine detail and description, you feel as if you are around a table hearing the stories told!

Herself a first-generation child of migrant parents, Zoe has captured the essence of the migrant experience as she recorded their stories, from fear and trepidation about leaving the home country; to celebrations; the first school day ever; to settling-in and to owning a business.

The stories are very relatable to all readers whether it be self-identity, intolerance, cultural misunderstandings, and environmental issues. There is a multitude of themes which can be used for discussions and writing. Learners will love chatting about it as they read the stories and relay their own experiences. The writing itself is easy to understand even if you have learning difficulties and Zoe has included pictures so that students can predict the context of the story before they read.

Zoe has been vigilant to ensure that the writing is *dyslexic friendly* such as making fonts appropriate. It is also chunked into short chapters, so it is not an overwhelming task to read. Further, Zoe has also included the number of words at the end of every story to promote the idea of success e.g., 'I have read this many words!'

Zoe, her family and her friends have co-jointly spent many hours recording these humorous and historical stories, so students can read along with them, refining their pronunciation and reading speed.

As a final touch, activities are included with answers at the end of the book which busy teachers can use, or students can use for self-study, which includes Aussie slang and figures of speech. Further study can be found in her four *Speak English like Australians! EAL/EFL Grammar & Activities Textbooks*.

Speak English like Australians – True Adventures of Aussie Kids with Migrant Parents, has it all – text that is easy to read, pictures and photos that will make you laugh, a dyslexic-friendly layout, themes for discussion, resources, and recordings of the stories. And what is more – they are all true!

Karen Dymke, Dec., 2023

About Karen

Consultant, Facilitator, Coach, International Specialised Skills Institute Fellow
https://thoughtfulworks.com.au/

"When I think of Karen, I think of innovation and energy." Karen is involved with: teacher education, presentations, facilitation, workshops, coaching, Think Tanks, project management, curriculum development, being an MC and creative ideas.

Karen is passionate about what she does as an educator, no matter what the context and has had the opportunity to work across all sectors and learn from each experience and now share practice. Karen keeps informed about the latest research into what progresses student learning and achievement and thinks it's a lot of fun when you learn.

sheep country: The green and gold colours of Australia are common in the counrty-side, around Hamilton.

the town of Hamilton in 1881
State Library of Victoria, http://handle.slv.vic.gov.au/10381/257676

Contents

Characters in the book...ii
Chapter 1	Coming to Australia	1
Chapter 2	Becoming an Aussie	11
Chapter 3	The Marriage Proposal	18
Chapter 4	Family	33
Chapter 5	School	41
Chapter 6	School Ceremonies and Routines	50
Chapter 7	Imperial Australia	58
Chapter 8	ANZAC Day	76
Chapter 9	Katie and The Beatles	82
Chapter 10	Music	88
Chapter 11	The Accident	96
Chapter 12	Celebrations	106
Chapter 13	Fun, Games and Pets	118
Chapter 14	At Home	128
Chapter 15	Obsessions and Hobbies	140
Chapter 16	The Woodshed	146
Chapter 17	The Hamilton Show	152
Chapter 18	Going for Sunday Drives	160
Chapter 19	Guy Fawkes Night	166
Chapter 20	Pets	172
Chapter 21	The Billy-Cart	186
Chapter 22	The Monorail	192
Chapter 23	Sticks and Stones	198
Chapter 24	The Pipe Tunnel and Prince	204
Chapter 25	The Bike	212
Chapter 26	The Bicycle Lesson	218
Chapter 27	The Childhood Home	222
Chapter 28	The First School Day Every Year	230
Chapter 29	Pleasures	238
Chapter 30	The Club	248
Chapter 31	The Sleepover	258
Chapter 32	New Beginnings	264

Voula, Jimmy and Peter in the Hamilton Botanical Gardens [about 1967]

Characters in the book

Theo is a migrant from Greece who arrived in Australia in 1953 and married Argyro in early 1956. He became the business partner of Andy Hadis who owned Lucas Café.

Andy Hadis owned Lucas Café from 1951 to 1969. He married Katina and had four children: Theo, Peggy, Steven and John.

Voula is the daughter of Theo and Argyro, Peter is their older son and Jimmy is the youngest child.

Bob Tydon is Peter's best friend who lived across the road from his house. He loves the Essendon football team and owns about 50 pigeons.

Don and Margaret Shmitz are next-door-neighbours of Theo and Argyro. They have three children.

Chapter 1
Coming to Australia

Theo wanted to help his mother, because his father had died when a boat he was travelling in, tipped over. His father was in the boat with his two grandchildren, who had been holidaying with their grandparents. Their grandfather was taking them back home to their parents when they all fell into the sea and all three died. The grandfather's body was never found, but the children's bodies were carried out of the sea and put on a cart pulled by a horse, for their last trip home. Theo was just twenty years old when that happened. He was the eldest son in the family, born in 1920. He had two brothers and three sisters. He had an older married sister, Panayiota married to Stavros, who owned a bakery in the city of Kalamata. Theo's father had sent him to the city of Kalamata to help out at his sister's bakery, without pay.

When the bodies of her two children arrived in the cart, Theo was there to see and to share his sister's grief and pain. The children's father, Stavros, was so shocked that he lost his mind and was put in hospital. He never got better! Now that his own father had died, Theo felt he had to find work to help support his family, but it was hard to find a job in Greece during and after the Second World War, in 1945. Then, something terrible happened! There was another war in Greece, from 1946 to 1949. It was a civil war between neighbours and brothers. This war was very bad and many Greeks killed each other. Even Theo had been captured and was a prisoner in a three-storey brick building. For some months, he was tied up and had to lay down on a concrete floor, to sleep. This gave him back pain, but he wasn't killed! They let him go free. Lucky!

After these wars Greece was a very poor country and the government had little control. Theo looked hard to find work and he felt fortunate when he got a job as a policeman, at about thirty years of age.

At that time, young men were walking around the streets of Athens wearing only one arm in their sleeve. The other sleeve was left empty! Maybe it was a new fashion, or maybe they were complaining about the government. The government wanted to stop young men from doing this. They gave all policemen a pair of scissors and told them to cut off empty sleeves. After being through wars, Theo thought this was a bit funny—when he used his scissors to cut the empty sleeves off jumpers and jackets. He didn't mind doing it.

Another thing the Greek Government wanted was to make sure cafes and restaurants were clean places. They ordered policemen to check the businesses that sold food. If a policeman found any dust, they had to give a warning to the owners. On the next visit, if the dust was still there, when the policeman came back to check, the business was closed down! Theo did not like doing this job. He did not like closing down shops and making it hard for people to run a business. Theo's job was a good

Theo arrived in Australia carrying only his passport, this small suitcase and a bit of money. He gave half of his money to a 19-year-old, Greek passenger from Kalamata. This hard-working teenager later opened a jewellery shop: Alex Brothers, in Lonsdale Street, Melbourne.

Landing: Passengers getting off a ship at Port Melbourne in 1954

The Sydney Morning Herald

Dutch migrants arriving in 1954

National Archives Australia

one and he got good money. But when he saw how unhappy people were, and how hard it was for them when he closed down their shops, Theo felt bad. He didn't want to do this work anymore, so he quit his job as a policeman!

By this time Theo was in his early thirties. He was tall, handsome and full

a railway line

of hope for the future. What could he do now to get some money? He had already helped his sisters find husbands and built houses for them, but now he wanted to help his two younger brothers. Theo knew the olive trees the family owned in their fields were not enough for all three brothers. When each brother got married and had kids, the olives and the oil, from the olive trees, would not bring in enough money. The olive trees were enough for only one family. Theo loved his brothers and decided to help them by leaving the fields for his two brothers. He decided to go overseas for a chance at a better life. Also he knew he would have a job and could send money back to his bothers and his mother. Many migrants had this idea. Theo did not really want to leave Greece but it would help his family to go and find work overseas. Where did he go? To Australia!

So, in October 1953, he got on the ship called *Fairstar*, which was going to Melbourne. That year, Theo was one of about 75,000 new migrants, who left with much hope, to live in Australia.

bark on the Black Wattle tree

Trains left from Station Pier taking migrants Bonegilla. [1950]
http://discover.bonegilla.org.au/

Block 4 of the Bonegilla camp in 1954 [one of 30 Migrant Hostels used in Australia at that time.]

English lessons at Bathurst Migrant Camp [1951]
National Archives of Australia

The Australian Government needed migrants, so it paid for Theo to go to Australia by ship. After that, Theo had to pay back the money by working for two years for the Australian Government. Theo had to work anywhere the government told him to go. He had to do any job the government needed to get done. It was called the *Assisted Passage Programme* because they helped people to go to Australia. These men, who came from Europe, built Australia. It was hard work. They built roads, railways, telephone lines, electricity and water dams.

When Theo arrived in Melbourne he was taken to a place called *Bonegilla*. Many migrants went there for two or three weeks to learn a bit of English until they got a job from the government. It is still there and is about 300 km north-east of Melbourne. Theo's first job was to make railway lines for the trains in Victoria. He *worked like a dog*, to show the men he was working with, that he was not lazy. However, the workers, who were all Australians, told him to take it easy. "Just relax a little," they told him. "Take it easy! There's no hurry!" That was the first time he heard the Australian idea of *taking it easy* and *she'll be right mate*. Theo soon learnt about tea-breaks and when it was time for a *smoko*. Theo's job was not easy, but everyone worked hard to build-up young Australia.

His next job was to take the bark off Black Wattle trees in Western Australia. The bark was used for burning and drying animal skins to make shoes. Some left-over bark was put on paths. "The Tan", the 4 km path around the Royal Botanic Gardens in Melbourne, got its name because tan bark was put on top of it.

When Theo finished his two years of work for the Government he went back to Melbourne. What job could he find? He took a train out of Melbourne to the end of the railway line. His journey ended in Hamilton, in the western part of Victoria. Theo had been to Hamilton before, so he knew 11,000 people lived there. (An ex-Prime Minister, Mr. Malcolm Fraser, lived on a farm there too.) It is a country place and everyone knows it has the best sheep in Australia: the Merino sheep. Hamilton has two main streets of shops: in Gray Street and in Thompson Street. Theo got off the train and walked along Gray Street and down Thompson Street, looking at the shops.

Working with Aussies, Theo had learnt to drink beer. He enjoyed drinking one or two glasses. When he saw the Commercial Hotel, he went in to buy a glass of beer. It felt good to be off the train and to sit in a cool place with other men. In those days it was against the law for women to drink at a pub: it was only for men.

As he was drinking his beer, he looked around and saw a man wink at him. Theo became very angry and his face turned a red colour. In his country, men only winked at women. Theo didn't want anyone to have any wrong ideas about him. He got up, walked to the man, and was going to punch him in his face! Quickly some men near there stopped him. They asked him what was wrong. With his little English Theo told them that the man had winked at him and that it was very rude! He was going to teach this man a lesson! The men explained to Theo that in Australia, a wink can sometimes mean "Good day!" or "How are you going mate?" Theo felt ashamed and said sorry to the man who had winked at him. They shook hands. It had all been a mistake because of their different cultures.

As Theo left the hotel he heard the men laughing at him. His face went red again. He knew he must learn many new things about life in Australia. After two years he still had a lot to learn. He must learn to speak English like Australians! It is true that when we don't know things, we make mistakes, but by mistakes we can also learn. Unlucky Theo thought he had heard "How are you going Mike?" After his mistake in the hotel, Theo usually said hello to people and winked at them too. To be extra friendly he often said, "How you going *Mike*?" All his life, Theo did not know it was "mate", because he thought he had heard "Mike". He just did not know the words were different. His future family did not correct him, because they thought it was his way of being funny! (1600 words)

the Hamilton Railway Station [2014]

an old wooden cart used to carry logs

Merino sheep with their wool cut off, in a paddock outside Hamilton

a beautiful sunset in Hamilton

The Commercial Hotel has not changed much.

the Greek flag on the roof of Lucas Cafe

Chapter 2
Becoming an Aussie

Theo left the hotel smiling to himself and shaking his head. Australia sure was a strange place! The people had different ways of doing things and food like olives and feta cheese were unavailable in the local shops, in 1953! In those days the Australian Government wanted migrants to change their cultures and become like other Australians. They did not want *New Australians* to keep their old cultures. Migrants had to change their old ways and fit in like everyone else. That was the law. Theo felt uncomfortable because his thinking and the Greek culture were different from the Aussie culture! He wanted to fit in, but it wasn't easy, because good things always take time.

As Theo walked down Gray Street, the main street, he felt hungry. Then he saw the "Lucas Café" sign. What he did not see was that there was a Greek flag flying on the roof of the shop.

Anyway, a nice smell came from the door. Theo knew the smell of "chips". He went inside to buy some. The shop was long and cool and there were tables and chairs on the left and right sides. At the front, beside the door there was a bench. Behind this bench Theo could see there were lollies, chocolates, cigarettes and ice-creams for sale. There was a man standing who was looking at him with interest. "Chips plis," said Theo. The man smiled at Theo's accent and asked him where he was from. They talked for a little time and got to know each other. The man behind the bench was Andy and he was the owner of Lucas Café. Andy was a Greek from Cyprus, a British Colony. His English was pretty good, because he learned it in Cyprus, in primary school. While they talked, Theo told Andy he needed a job. Lucky for Theo, Andy needed a worker and gave Theo a job, peeling potatoes and helping in the kitchen.

After a few months, Theo was chopping potatoes and grilling steaks like an expert! As the months passed, Andy's two business partners left the café to live in Melbourne. When this happened, Theo asked to be Andy's new partner and a part owner of the business. Andy, who spoke good English would be the front man speaking with the customers, while Theo would do most of the cooking and cleaning at the back of the shop. (The two men worked well together for fifteen years, before the shop closed.)

The café was very busy and Theo had to work long hours: from 7 or 8am until 8 or 9pm. By the time he had cleaned up and locked up the shop, he sometimes didn't get home till 10pm! Theo always walked home, about 900 metres. He could not drive and the cool night air felt good, after working inside all day. Theo lived with Andy and his small family in French Street, across the road from the Botanical Gardens.

Theo was doing well in his new country. He was trying to be like an Aussie and learn about the Aussie culture.

the house in French Street opposite the Botanical Gardens

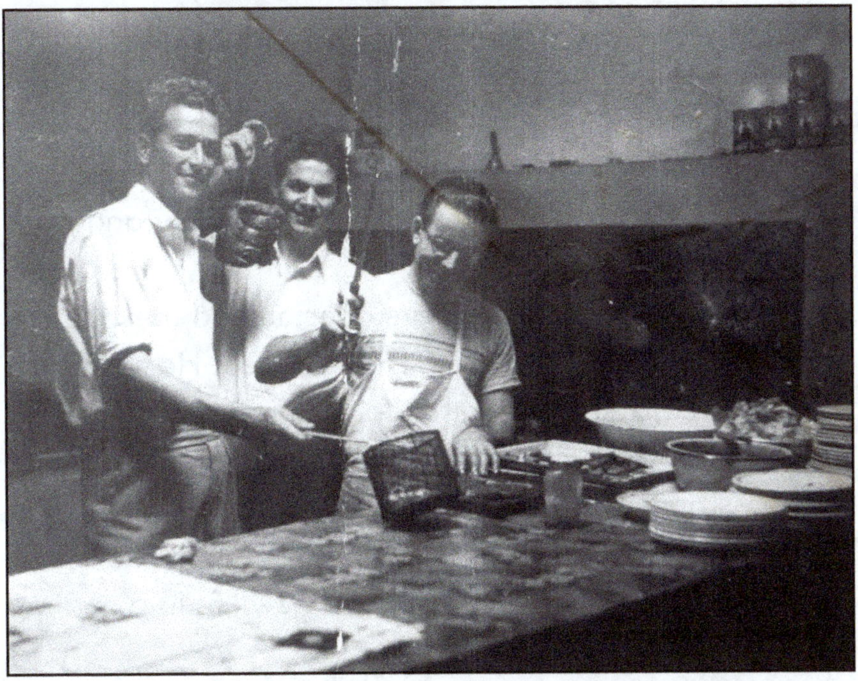

Theo, Andy and an old business partner in the café kitchen

But something was missing! He did not feel okay with his life! He was feeling alone. He found he was always thinking about a lovely girl, Argyro, he had met in Greece. He had only spoken to her a few times. She had not flirted with him as some girls did. Theo remembered the funeral of her uncle when he spoke to her and she was serious and polite. She was also beautiful. He had thought about marrying her, but he did not ask her to marry him, because her family was very poor. He did not have much money to take a wife. In those days a girl needed a *dowry* to help her marry. Theo had worked hard in Greece to give two of his sisters dowries so they could find husbands. At that time he thought it was right to get a dowry himself, from his wife's family. In the villages of Kalamata where he had lived, the dowry custom was common. Everyone gave dowries to their daughters. But poor Argyro had no dowry.

What was Argyro like? She was honest, hard-working and nine years younger than Theo. She was of average height and build. Her hair was shortish, wavy and dark brown. Her eyes were hazel.

Now in Australia, four years after he had met Argyro, Theo wanted to start a family. He felt lonely. He wanted to write a letter to Argyro's father to ask him a question. Did Argyro want to come to Australia to get married to him? By now Theo did not want a dowry, but would Argyro leave her country, and all the people she loved to marry him? Would she take a chance at a new life in a strange country? (809 words)

Argyro at 25 and 17 years old

the gates of the Botanical Gardens'

Not long after arriving in Australia, Theo, second left, is enjoying his glass of beer and a lunch with other Greeks in Hamilton.

Argyro's uncle, Captain Panos Katsareas was killed by guerillas in the civil war in Greece, in 1947. Theo had spoken to her at this uncle's memorial service.

Chapter 3
The Marriage Proposal

Theo decided to write a letter to Argyro's father. He wrote that he wanted to marry his daughter. Theo respected her father as he knew he was a strict dad. Would he allow his daughter to go to Australia? Would Argyro be willing to leave her family? Theo did not know the Australian Government wanted to get more white people into Australia. The Government wanted the single migrant men who worked in Australia, to stay in Australia and to have families. So the Government paid, for single women from places like Greece and Italy, to come to Australia to get married to these men. Theo didn't know about this government plan, so he sent money to Argyro's father, for a one-way ticket by ship. He hoped Argyro would take the money and come to Australia to be his wife.

But, during this time Argyro had left her village and moved to the capital city, Athens. She lived in a flat with her older brother, Nick, who was a student at the university there. Athens was a busy city and Argyro loved the city life and noise, as there was always something to see and do.

Because Argyro wanted to learn how to make clothes, she studied very hard at a sewing school in Athens. She loved sewing and pattern-making. Everything the teacher showed her was easy for her, and she was the best student

Argyro (right) walking with classmates

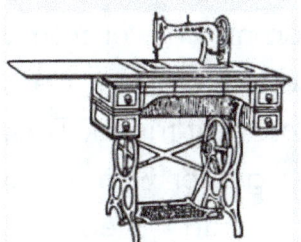

A treadle sewing machine, used at that time, was operated with the foot.

Athens in the early 1950s

in her class.

When Argyro's father told her that Theo was asking to marry her, it was very difficult for her to make a decision. Argyro enjoyed her life in Athens and she didn't want to leave her country. She knew she would miss her family and she loved her studies and her new friends. Athens was an interesting city after the slow, boring farming life she had in her village.

Time moved on and she still didn't know what to do. She put it all in the "too hard basket", so she did not give an answer to Theo, who was waiting in Australia. Argyro forgot that delay is the thief of time! In Australia, after *six months* of waiting, Theo still had no answer from Argyro! What was going on? Theo needed to know. He wrote to his cousin Ilias, who was also his best friend. Theo asked Ilias to go to Argyro and talk together with her, face-to-face, about going to Australia to marry Theo.

To speak to Argyro and get an answer for Theo as soon as he could, kind Ilias left for the city that same day. He knew where Argyro was living, because Argyro's brother was his friend and everyone knows each other's business in the small village where they lived. In Athens, Argyro's mother was visiting them for a few weeks. When Ilias arrived at the flat in Athens, Argyro saw him through her window. She knew Ilias and Theo were closer than brothers. She told her mother that she thought Ilias wanted to talk to her about Theo and she was right! Ilias told her that Theo was worrying and waiting for her reply.

Argyro felt ashamed because she had not answered him for such a long time. She told Ilias that she had

Argyro is seen 2nd left in the back row, with her family soon after World War 2.

already written to Theo "yesterday", saying she would marry him. It was a lie of course! Ilias felt happy and he was sure Theo would be full of joy! He did think it was very good luck that Argyro wrote her letter just one day before his visit! It was great news for Theo!

The truth was that Argyro wrote the letter to Theo the *next* day and posted it. Now her decision was finally made, she was going to keep her promise. After the Second World War, most Europeans were poor and sadly for the women, there were not many young men left alive to marry. Also, many young, unemployed men left Europe to find work overseas in the USA or Australia.

As already mentioned, Argyro's family was poor, and her parents had nine children to care for. Argyro, the second oldest, felt she must help them. She knew it would be easier for her mum and dad if she left for Australia to get married. But she really *didn't want* to leave her country. She loved Greece, yet she was the one in her family who must leave it! Concern for her family made her leave her people and her country! Just like Theo had already done before her, Argyro decided to migrate to help her family. Argyro did know a bit about Theo. She had seen him and spoken to him maybe four or five times. She had heard other girls gossiping about him and hoping to meet him.

She had spoken to Theo when he came to the funeral of her mother's brother, who had been killed in the civil war, in March '47. She loved her uncle very much and was depressed when he had died. She remembered that her uncle played with her when she was just a small girl. He had let her boss him and make him do whatever she said. Often she had wanted to go on his strong shoulders, and to order him where to take her; treating him like her horse! Then, when she was seventeen, he was shot and killed by the enemy on a quiet mountain road. He was only thirty-three years old. It was at this loved uncle's funeral service that Theo had first spoken to her. Argyro had worn black mourning clothes. She was serving coffee and dry biscuits. She knew Theo liked her serious manner, and her sad eyes had touched his heart. Theo was a young soldier, and her uncle had been his captain. "Who is your father?" Theo had asked her. Now she was going to Australia, a strange and wealthy land, to marry Theo. She did not know him well. What a thing to happen! She hoped to be lucky and happy with her new life in Australia.

Over the next few weeks, she cried till her eyes were red. She knew she would not see her family for many, many years. To tell the truth, it took Argyro twenty-one years before she went back to Greece for a visit. In those days Australia was *at the ends of the earth*, and nobody in Greece knew much about it. No one had a television or a computer. Telephones calls were very expensive too.

However, it took another one and a half years before she got her visa, because Theo did not know what to do and what paperwork was needed. After many efforts, and mistakes with government people, and with Andy's help, Theo at last sent her a ticket to Australia! Theo's brother, Punuyiotis, came to see her leave at the port, at Pireaus, where big passenger ships left Greece. He tried to cheer her up by making her think of her future. "I want to hear that you have had a son," he told her.

As the ship left the port, Argyro cried because she was leaving her life behind. Suddenly she felt scared: what was she doing leaving her country? She ran to the highest part of the ship at the back, to see her last view of her much loved Greece. She wanted her brothers and sisters to see her, so she took off her brown coat and waved it

Punuyiotis tells Argyro, "I want to hear you have had a son."

to them like a flag. She stood there waving her coat until she couldn't see them anymore. Then she slowly walked to her shared room on the ship.

In those days flying on an airplane cost a lot, so most emigrants travelled by ship and shared rooms as well. In the 1950's, the Immigration Department of Australia, brought to Australia many ships full of young European women. These young ladies wanted to marry the migrant men already working in Australia. The ships were called "bride ships". Argyro was on a bride ship called the *Tasmania*. It had been built to transport cows, but now it carried 800 women! They were all going to Australia with the idea of getting married and starting families in their new country. The Australian Government wanted to get more people to live in Australia. To help the young men stay in Australia, the Government gave free transport for these women. But Theo didn't know about this and he paid for Argyro's fare himself, as already mentioned.

The first part of Australia that Argyro saw was Fremantle, Western Australia. Some of the women were meeting their future husbands here. Near the port, the women on the *Tasmania* saw many small boats filled with men. They had come out on boats to welcome the women. Many were holding flowers for the ladies and calling out to them.

All the future brides got off to walk on land for the first time in three weeks. They soon saw a café and went inside to get a drink of water. The only thing they really wanted was to taste fresh tap water, because the water on the ship was not very nice! However, they couldn't speak

English and the café worker couldn't understand Greek. Since the café worker was British, he gave them cups of tea! Greek people don't really like tea much, and the women felt unhappy because they could not get a simple thing like water! This was the first time they could not understand English, and they realised that life would not be easy in Australia. Thankfully, someone called out the word "water" and soon some wonderful water, sweeter than honey, was given to them at last.

After staying in Fremantle for only a few hours, the *Tasmania* arrived in Melbourne five days later. The whole trip from Greece had taken 28 days! What a welcome waited for the women on the ship! Hundreds of happy and excited young men were cheering and whistling, as they waited on the wharf. Many carried bunches of flowers and there were ribbons of coloured paper everywhere. The hopes and dreams of hundreds of young men and women were about to come true. But not for all! Many faces searched for each other.

Italian women on board a "bride ship" 1954

streamers like cobwebs, as passengers and friends greet one another

Some women had never met their future husbands, and held black and white photos of them in their nervous hands. Some women were not happy when they met their men, and returned to Greece without getting married! Others had a nice surprise. Argyro was lucky because she had already met Theo, even though she had only spoken a few times to him. She didn't really know him very well though, so she feared for her future. She missed the voices of her family and friends.

Theo had sent Argyro a photo of himself too, but she hated how he looked in it. She thought he looked angry and harsh. She didn't like to look at it. For this reason, when her roommates had shown photos of their future husbands to each other, during their long voyage, Argyro had not. As girls usually do, they had asked Argyro, "Is he handsome? Is he tall or short?" Argyro had replied, "He is an old man." (He was nine years older than she was.) So they didn't talk to her about it again. The other girls felt sorry for her because they thought poor Argyro was going to marry a really old man. Argyro felt lonely and she often cried because she had left her family and country.

Now, finally in Melbourne the women were looking down from the ship at the men. Argyro's roommates called out to her. "Can you see your Theo? Is he here?" Argyro pointed to a very tall, good-looking man in his early thirties. He was dressed in a suit and he was holding a bunch of red roses. They were amazed! "Oh, you were joking, he is not old at all. He is really a very handsome, *young* man!" they said, laughing. They felt happy for her.

"Good luck for your future. Goodbye! Goodbye!" The date was January 4th, 1956.

There were only a few Greek churches in Melbourne, so it was a very busy time. There were so many couples wanting to get married in a hurry. Argyro and Theo had to wait, so they got married at a government registry office. The day after that, they left Melbourne to go to Hamilton. They took a copy of their marriage certificate with them. In March, Theo invited a Greek Orthodox priest to come and marry them in Hamilton in a Church of England church, because there were no Greek churches in Hamilton.

Theo was a generous man. He also wanted to please his new wife, so he hired a taxi to drive the priest all the way from Melbourne to Hamilton, 300km. It cost a lot of money! So the next morning, Theo made a quick decision to put the priest on a plane for his return trip to Melbourne, since it would be cheaper than a taxi. Andy Hadis drove the priest to the Hamilton Aerodrome. Theo and Argyro went along too, just for company even though they were still in their pyjamas. Unluckily, they were late and the plane had already gone. The priest missed his flight. Next the priest decided to drive the car himself, all the way back to Melbourne! After that, still dressed in their pyjamas, they all drove back to Hamilton, because they needed to open the café the next day. What a very long day it had been! (2260 words)

Argyro's glory box came with her on the ship. Inside were woven blankets from her village, tablecloths and her best clothes.

Argyro and her bridemaids enter the car to travel to the Church of England "half a k" up the road!

They made a lovely couple on their wedding day. Argyro wore a beautiful bridal-gown they bought from Rockmans, a dress shop in Hamilton. It was covered in beautiful French lace.

the photo of Theo that Argyro didn't like

inside the Anglican Church, 22 Gray Street, Hamilton

Argyro, on her wedding day, is with her bridesmaid Mary and her friend, also named Argyro. They had all met in Hamilton.

Argyro's home was built by her father with the help of his kids. Made of stone it took over 20 years of work. Under the house there was space to house hens, goats and sheep. On their land they grew wheat and they also owned an olive grove.

Hamilton is about 300km west of Melbourne.

Argyro's village, Saint Nikonas is in Mani, south of Sparti, on the mountains near the southern coastline. The people are known for their independence and toughness; it was from there the uprising started on 6/3/1821 againt the 400 year Turkish occupation. The World Factbook

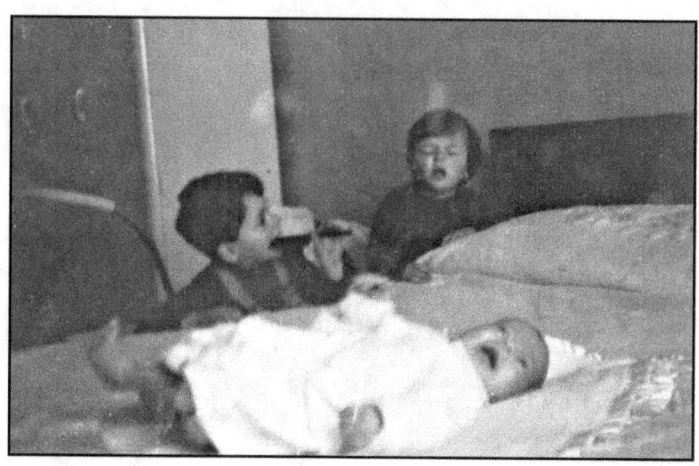

The family became complete in 1960 with the birth of "The Baby", Jimmy.

Argyro sewed lovely clothes for her children. She had a penchant for flowers, so she gave Voula a rose to hold. Flowers often featured in Argyro's photos!

Chapter 4
Family

In March 1956 the Olympic Games came to Melbourne and Australians were excited about the fast runner, John Landy. When he ran his famous trial race, all of Australia wanted him to win. However during this race, at Olympic Park in Melbourne, he stopped to help a young runner, Ron Clarke, who had fallen. But John Landy did not give up and he started running the race again. He ran so fast that he won the race, even though he had stopped to help someone else! Because of John Landy's kind behaviour, people started calling him Gentleman Landy. He had won the hearts, not only of all Australians, but of the rest of the world, because of his kind and respectful attitude!

Argyro didn't go to the Olympics. She stayed in Hamilton, trying hard to get used to living there after her life in Greece. It was a country town so there were no English classes to help her. Anyway, everyone thought a migrant would somehow learn English by themselves, and would accept the Aussie way of doing things. Also, Australians were not interested in other cultures. Migrants had to become *New Australians* and had to change their "old" way of life. Furthermore, because most Australians did not understand other cultures, they were impatient with migrants. "Go back to where you came from!" they sometimes told migrants, or "Speak English like Australians!"

In those days, British culture was common and taught in schools. Australians loved everything about England, which was the "motherland". There was a law called *The White Australia Policy* that encouraged white migrants, and especially British immigrants, to migrate to Australia. From 1944 to 1949 a British citizen living in Australia, automatically became an Australian citizen! That is how important Britain was to Australia.

Hamilton Hospital

Anyway, Argyro became pregnant soon after her marriage. She went to hospital to have her first child. Sadly, it was a difficult time for her because she didn't know much English. When the nurses tried to tell her things, poor Argyro did not understand at all! She was very scared! She also felt ashamed that she didn't speak English. Argyro wished she could understand what the nurses were telling her to do! To make things worse, men were not allowed to be with their wives during the birth, so Theo waited in another room for news of his wife and baby. In his heart, he probably wanted a son to continue the family name. It was a very important part of his culture. Theo wanted to name his future son "Peter" after his own father, who had passed away when Theo was just nineteen. To give his father's name, to his own son, was a way he could honour his father's memory.

Argyro gave birth to a perfect, tiny baby girl. Argyro remembered the last words of her brother-in-law, "I want to hear you have had a son!" She wished she had given her husband a son. She was very upset, because she knew Theo wanted a boy. After the birth, Theo was taken by a nurse to see his daughter in the nursery. He could not help feeling disappointed, but he was a practical man. He soon pushed away his negative thoughts. When Theo was allowed to see his wife, Argyro thought she saw his disappointment. She started to cry and refused to take her newborn daughter from the nurse. Argyro felt very confused, homesick and hurt. However, the nurse thought Argyro did not understand, and she put the small baby into Argyro's arms. Argyro's attitude changed as she held her daughter. Theo encouraged his wife by telling her that this was their child, and they would love

Peter is standing in the front yard of the beautiful Victorian-era house next door to Gray Street State School. Notice the water tap is turned fully on as there were no water restrictions. Over the fence was Gray Street State School.

her very much. Theo really did love his daughter, naming her Voula, after his mother. He thought that maybe the next child would be a son....

In fact, there were soon more mouths to feed and the next two babies were both sons, Peter and Demetrius (Jimmy), so Theo and Argyro were happy that they had "done their duty" and the family name could continue. Later in life they would have a grandson named Theo, born to their first son, Peter. So the tradition of family names continued unbroken.

Argyro taught her children the Greek language and culture. She still missed her family in Greece, so it helped her to talk to her small children about them. By this time, Theo had moved his young family into a rental house next door to the local primary school. Hamilton had some beautiful houses and this one was a large house with high ceilings and a big, heavy-wooden front door.

Everything was going well for the little family. But, accidents always happen! One day their little son, Peter, got his hand squashed when the heavy, front door closed on it. Argyro didn't know what to do to help take away Peter's pain. She did what the old women in her village had done. She chopped up onions, added oil and vinegar, put it all on a towel, and then wrapped up his injured hand with the towel for a bandage. It was to help take away the bruising. Anyway, Peter's hand got better!

Because of the primary school next door, little Peter and Voula could hear a lot of interesting noises coming from over the fence. It was a mixture of yelling, laughing children at play. Peter and Voula sometimes stood on chairs, to look over the fence, at the primary school children playing in the school yard. But the school children teased them and were not very kind at all. They thought Pete and Voula were *busybodies*, sticking their noses over the fence and looking at them! Also Voula and Pete didn't seem very friendly, because they wouldn't speak to the Aussie school kids. There were three reasons why. Firstly, they were too shy; secondly, they couldn't speak much English and lastly they were only two and three years old and didn't know much! (998 words)

a stately home opposite the Botanical Gardens near where Theo lived with his family

Some homes can be seen that are not so grand! Here is a very old cottage that still stands in Hamilton, perhaps dating back to the 1850s. [2007]

Theo and Argyro, with their daughter, Voula. She is wearing the rust-coloured coat mentioned in chapter 3.

Posing are Theo and Argyro, after three years of marriage.

Voula and Peter at play, next door to the school

After sharing a house with the Hadis family for about a year, Theo moved his family to their second share house. Here Argyro, left, is sitting on the grass with baby Voula.

[They later moved into a rental property, next-door to Gray Street State School, for about two years, before buying the Byron Street house for £5,000 in cash.]

standing in front of the "veggie patch" soon after moving to their own place in Byron Street

Voula, Argyro and Peter in the Hadis' garden

Chapter 5
School

Finally, the day arrived when Voula reached the age of five and started preps. She found primary school was a strange new world of *blah, blah, blah!* Voula learnt that she had to be quiet and not speak until the teacher asked her a question. That was not a problem, since she couldn't speak much English at all! Everything she learned was by copying what the other kids did in class. If they stood up behind their little chairs, so did Voula. If they walked to the front of the class and sat on little mats, so did Voula too. Everything seemed very different. She thought the teachers were very tall and strict, especially when they stood on the platform in front of the blackboard. Voula felt different from her classmates, even though she wore a school uniform like them. She was unlike the other kids because of her olive skin and she had no freckles like a lot of the sun-burnt English kids.

Things got worse. One day, Argyro decided to shave off *all* of Voula's hair with a razor, to make it thicker. Argyro thought it was too thin and that it was nice for girls to have lots of lovely, thick hair! Well! Voula had an even more difficult time at school, because at playtime the children pulled off her little beanie to laugh at her bald, shiny head. All of these differences separated Voula

The three siblings: Voula is in her school uniform and by the end of 1961 her hair had grown back.

Argyro shaved Voula's hair and gave her a beanie to wear for the first few months, to protect her from the cold.

author's own photos

from her classmates. None of the other kids wanted to be friends with such a strange girl!

The children learnt to read from a "reader" called *John and Betty*. Everyone had their own book and took it home to practise reading. In class, Voula took her turn going to the teacher's desk, to read *John and Betty* out loud to her. She read one or two pages per day and when she got to the end she read it again, until she could read it quickly. (Then she got her next reader, which was more difficult.)

The readers were about the traditional, middle-class lives of girls and boys in Britain: boys played with trains and girls with tea-sets. After a year Voula was able to understand quite a bit of English. When the children teased her and said they could "boss her around," Voula replied with, "No, you can't!" Her answer only made them tease her more by saying, "You don't even know what that means!" Voula replied, "Yes I do!" The other kids yelled, "Go on then, show us!" So Voula took a girl by the hand and pulled her around and around herself, in a circle. That is what she understood by "boss around". Of course the children laughed at her and Voula felt afraid and alone. Most children like to feel they belong and are friends with their classmates. Nowadays, schools have rules against bullying, but even so, it is still around in schools. It seems that children can be very cruel to one another!

Not many *New Australians* lived in Hamilton in those days. Probably there are still not too many there today either. Life was tough for them because they were not accepted by many Aussies. In those days there were no pizzas, olives, Feta cheese, delicatessens or newspapers printed in other languages. There were no McDonald's or Pizza Huts either. The Australian Government expected New Australians to magically become Aussies, forgetting their own cultures. It was different then; many people were racists and there were no laws against racism. There were no English language schools either. So, when Peter and Voula started school they had a difficult time, because other children called them rude names and wouldn't let them join in with their games at playtime. Therefore, Theo and Argyro decided to send their younger son, Jimmy, to kindergarten, to give him a *head-start* with the Aussie culture. Neither Voula nor Peter had gone to kindergarten, but it was a good idea, because by the time Jimmy started primary school, he had made many friends and was accepted by his play-mates. He could also speak English like them.

When they were all at school, Jimmy, Peter and Voula walked to the café every day during their lunchtime. It was only a block away, so it took them five or ten minutes to get there: a shorter time when they ran. You can imagine the nice hot meals they enjoyed at Lucas Café. So, while their classmates ate Vegemite sandwiches the three siblings ate steak, chips and salad. Sometimes they had time for ice-cream and jelly, or fruit salad for dessert! The other children always wanted to know what Peter, Jimmy and Voula had for lunch: they were a bit jealous.

But when Voula was in grade three, it was her job to take little Jimmy to kinder three days a week, during her lunch-break. You see, by then, Argyro couldn't take him to kindergarten, because she was too busy working as a waitress at Lucas Café; lunch was their busiest time and they were "flat-out".

Voula took Jimmy's hand and they would walk from Lucas Cafe to his kinder. She tried to make her little brother hurry up by pulling him by the hand as they walked along. But, little Jimmy couldn't walk very fast and Voula was often late on those days, returning to her school after lunch.

After lunchtime, the school sometimes had assemblies, when all the school news was told to the teachers and kids by the headmaster. For Voula, the most embarrassing times were when the whole school was outside, in the yard, having Afternoon Assembly. When she was late, assembly had started. All the teachers and kids saw her as she ran through the gate, for about 75 metres, to join her class. It was her public shame! Especially because the students were told that it was important to be on time!

The headmaster, Mr. Harris was a short, plump, balding, kind-looking man, but he also knew how to be stern. Voula was scared of him and often felt her heart beating very fast and her face become red, as she ran into the school yard, after taking Jimmy to kindergarten.

Many times she was late, in front of everyone! She always felt terrible as she ran to her class group and joined them! Voula wanted to hide from everyone but she could not, as we cannot hide from ourselves. Each time it happened she promised herself she would never, ever be late again, but sadly.....without success! The teachers were not very kind about her problem and often scolded

her for being late. (1102 words)

in black, the route from primary school to kinder

Jimmy, in grade 2, is listening to the Infant Mistress, Miss Malcolm, reading a story. He is near her left arm looking at the book.
[The Spectator, 13 May 1967]

The family in the summer of 1963 is posing in front of the apple tree, while on the left, outside the outdoor laundry, is the replaced old "copper" used to boil water for washing clothes.

Argyro, Andy Hadis and Theo standing outside Lucas Café in the mid 1960s.

Chapter 6
School Ceremonies and Routines

At Hamilton's Gray Street State School, every Monday morning was Monday Assembly Day. The whole school got together to hear what the Headmaster had to say to them. However, the preps, grades 1 and grades 2 did not have the patience or the strength to stand up for a long time, so they had their own assemblies. They sat together in a big room, on little mats, and learnt songs and nursery rhymes with actions. Nursery rhymes like: "Incy Wincy Spider climbed the water spout." and "Mary, Mary quite contrary. How does your garden grow?" It was fun! Those who want to sing always find a song, and it gladdens their hearts.

Assembly seemed quite long to the older pupils, as they gathered in their grades and waited in a big U-shape, on the netball court, in front of the school. On the left side of the school was a flagpole and every year a sixth-grade boy had the pleasure of slowly raising the Australian flag while the school sang the Australian National Anthem. Australia's population was between ten and eleven million and most people were from Britain. In 1947, the population was 90% British, in 1988 it was 74.55%, in 1999 it was 69.88% and in 2021 it had reduced to 39.8%. So, back to the 1960s, Australians sang the *British National Anthem* as their own. On the next page are the

Mr. Harris, the
Headmaster of State
School No. 295

Gray Street State School as it stands today, little altered from the 1960s, except for the position of the flagpoles.

The National Anthem

God save our gracious Queen! Long live our no-ble queen!

God save the Queen! Send her vic- tor- i- ous, ha- ppy and glo- ri-ous

Lo-ng to re-ign o- ver us God save the Queen!

words and music of the first part of the National Anthem, which was the only one the children learnt.

Singing the anthem was a very important part of school life. It was an honour and a duty to show respect to your country. Children and adults stood up whenever the National Anthem was played at any public event. Voula certainly felt proud to be part of this ceremony. It was taken very seriously and the children had to show respect by standing straight, with feet together, and looking forward at the flag. No speaking or moving around was allowed, or the children would be punished.

Furthermore, to make sure the students sang very well together, the school recorder band played the music for the National Anthem. Just before the recorder band started, a boy who stood next to the flagpole, played his drum to introduce the singing. All the other kids were jealous of the drum boy! Everyone felt he had the best job in the school,... except for the boy who pulled the flag up to the top of the flagpole! *That* boy had the best job of all! Immediately after the anthem, the boys saluted the flag and the girls curtsied, holding their skirts.

A General Assembly was sometimes held after lunch. The children assembled in their grades again, on the netball court, to listen to important information that the teachers wanted to tell them. Also it was a time to announce the names of hard-working and good students. When these students went out to the front, the Head Master shook their hands, congratulated and thanked them and then everyone clapped for them. It was for these assemblies that Voula was often late, because of taking Jimmy to kindergarten during her lunchtime. One summer day, poor Voula had just run all the way back to school from kinder, without being too late. As she stood under the hot sun, she started feeling dizzy, her knees started to feel wobbly and she heard ringing in her ears: that was the first time in her life that she fainted! Luckily she didn't hurt herself as she fell over the children near her before she hit the ground.

Also after the raising of the flag, the children placed their right hands on their hearts and recited the Patriotic Declaration:

"I love God and my country. I honour the flag, I will serve the Queen, and cheerfully obey my parents, teachers and the law." Not many schools say this anymore, and even the *Oath of Allegiance,* for Australia's new citizens has been replaced by the *Australian Citizenship Pledge.* The pledge is taken by migrants becoming Australian Citizens, during Citizenship Ceremonies. They promise to respect their new country and its laws. Here is the pledge they say when they become Australian Citizens:

"From this time forward, (under God), I pledge my loyalty to Australia and its people, whose democratic beliefs I share, whose rights and liberties I respect, and whose laws I will uphold and obey." The Government Immigration website says:

"Repeating this pledge is the final step in becoming an Australian Citizen. By repeating the pledge, new citizens are making a formal and public commitment to Australia, including the responsibilities and privileges of citizenship." <http://www.immi.gov.au/>

Back in the 60s, after the pledge, the Gray Street State School students sometimes sang their *school song*. They needed to practise, so they could sing it when they had sports competitions with other schools. It helped to join together the spirits of all the kids. It must have been successful, because the school had a proud history of winning trophies and medals. On the wall outside Mr. Harris' office, there was a list of students' names who were champions. Here are some of the words of the school song:

"We girls and boys of Gray Street,
Hamilton 295,
We work and play together, ..."
"In basketball and swimming,
We always do our best..."

The school had four Sports Houses, named after native Australian birds: the Kookaburras, the Magpies, the Wrens and the Cockatoos. All the children of a family were put in the same House, so there would be no fighting. Jimmy, Peter and Voula were Kookaburras. Sometimes the School Houses would assemble on the four corners of the front school-ground. Each House went to a separate corner. Then marching music would be played over the Public Address System, (the PA). It was in 4/4 time. Each child in each House stretched out their arms to make straight lines with the child in front and beside them. They made perfect columns and rows. Then the children who were the House Captains called out, "Left, right, left, right, left, left ...," until everyone helped each other to lift the same leg at the same time. They all marched on the spot, with their arms swinging and looking straight ahead, until ordered to go. Each House group marched to the next corner of the grounds and then they had to turn the corner without losing their neat order of straight lines. It was a good exercise to work together and to help one another.

It was very enjoyable to spend some time marching. The winner was the House that marched the best as decided by the judges: usually the senior teachers. Each house was given points which went towards the end-of-year score and were part of the House Sports' scores. House Sports included an Athletics Carnival and a Swimming Carnival every year. Voula always came second or third in running, because two tall girls, Julie and Meagan, always beat her. Voula didn't know about training and did not discipline herself to practise, so she never actually came first, although she tried very hard on the day of the event. Maybe the *butterflies in her tummy* made her lose!

Another important routine at school was the drinking of free milk. All primary schools kids got milk to drink for free. It came in a half-pint glass bottle and was fresh, full-cream, dairy milk. Every day, just before morning playtime, the class Milk Monitors would go to collect a crate of milk bottles for their grade. Back in the class, they had the fun of using a pointy wooden stick to put holes in all the aluminium lids and then to put straws through the

Voula had butterflies in her tummy!

holes. When the milk bottles were ready, the class walked past and each child took a bottle, went back to their seat, and happily drank up the creamy milk. Sometimes the crates of bottles were forgotten out in the sun for too long and they were a bit warm, but everyone still drank their milk. People did not know about lactose allergies back then, and no one was allowed out to play until they had drunk up all their milk! (1369 words)

the front school grounds were full of marching children

a milk bottle with an aluminium foil lid

a kookaburra

a magpie

a cockatoo

a wren

Chapter 7
Imperial Australia

Today was April 17th, 1965, the day after Good Friday. Theo's and Argyro's three children were waiting for the bakery van to bring their Hot Cross Buns. Argyro had gone to the bakery two weeks ago, to order them. Now, the day was here for the buns to be delivered to their house. The Kings Bakery, in Brown Street, is still there, opposite Melville Oval in Hamilton. Many businesses are still owned by well-known local families. Back then in Australia, there were no fast food places like McDonald's. You could not go shopping any time you felt like it. There was no late night shopping either. When the shops closed at 5:30pm, you had to wait till the next day

Kings Bakery 1955
[photo supplied by Jan Franklyn - nee King]

Besides using a delivery van, Kings Bakery also used a horse and carriage to deliver buns well into the 1970s.
[photo supplied by Jan Franklyn - nee King]

to buy what you wanted. Even nowadays, shopping hours in Hamilton are from 9am to 5:30pm Monday to Friday and from 9am to 12pm on Saturday. Shops do not open at all on Sunday, which is *the day of rest*. Some shops now, do have late trading hours. The first fast food store to open in Australia was *Kentucky Fried Chicken,* in Sydney in 1968. Kentucky Fried Chicken was also the first fast food store to open in Hamilton. Everyone saw the advertising on TV that said the chicken was "finger-licking-good".

On the Saturday that the children waited for the bakery van, the shops closed at noon. So, the bakery truck driver wanted to deliver all his buns before noon too. The three kids knew their buns would come some time in the morning. Their noses were on the lounge window, as they looked for the van. They loved the delicious buns as they were a special treat. They only got *one* Hot Cross Bun every year, for Easter. Hot Cross Buns were as precious

Kings Bakery 2014

as gold! As they looked out onto the front street they saw the bakery van pull up in front of their house, so they excitedly called their mother. Argyro went to the door to greet the man and get the paper bag of Hot Cross Buns. When the children received their buns, they looked at them, and sniffed their sultana and cinnamon smell.

What each child tried to do was to make their bun last for as long as possible! Voula did what many children still do. She gently peeled off the white cross first, to eat it last; then the sultanas she could see at the top, sides and bottom were pulled off and chewed one by one, to

a penny

a thru'pence (three pence)

enjoy the sticky sweetness of their juices. Lastly, she pulled the bun apart in thin ribbons, and held them above her mouth, before she ate them, piece by piece.

In schools around Australia children were taught to look forward to these buns as part of Easter. They were a reminder of what Jesus Christ did for us when He died on the cross, and it was a celebration of his rising from death on the third day. That is the reason for the white cross on top of the buns. They were often served hot with butter spread on top. The tradition of Hot Cross Buns began in England, in the nineteenth century. Usually they were sold by street sellers who called out, "Hot Cross Buns" as people walked by.

While in primary school, Jimmy, Voula and Peter, along with thousands of other children across Australia, learned to sing a special nursery rhyme. The words go

Hot Cross Buns

like this:

> *Hot Cross Buns! Hot Cross Buns!*
> *One a penny two a penny – Hot Cross Buns*
> *If you have no daughters, give them to your sons*
> *One a penny two a penny – Hot Cross Buns!*

In 1965, the money used in Australia was the same as the British money: pennies, shillings and pounds. When Voula was in grade 3, in 1965, she learned about the British money and weights by memory. Also, primary school kids memorised up to the 12 times tables.

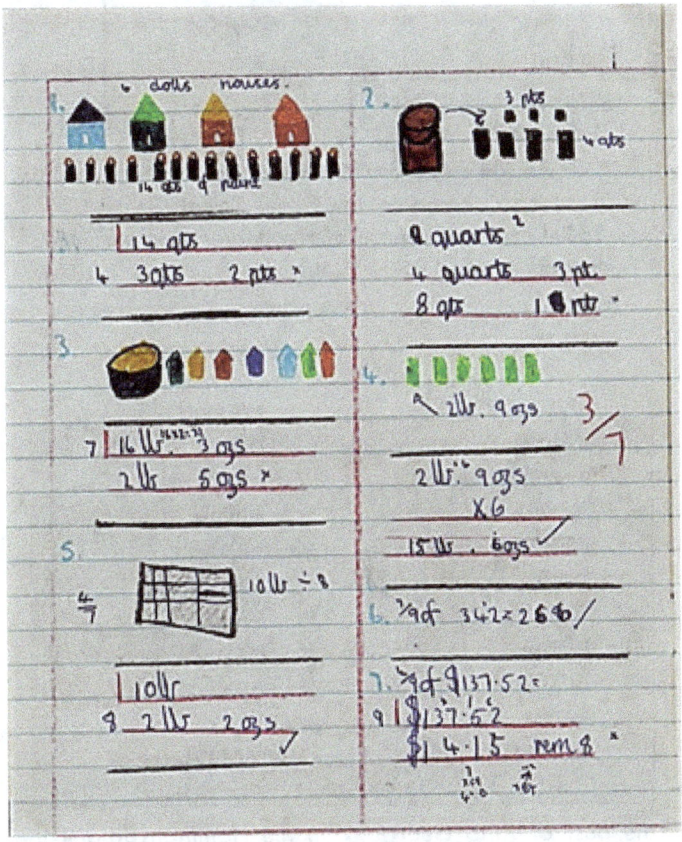

a grade 3 arithmetic exercise showing pounds and ounces

Most classrooms of Gray Street State School had a photo of Her Majesty on the wall. [circa 1950]

the bust of King George V in the Hamilton Botanical gardens

However, on the 14th February, 1966, the "old money" was taken away by the banks fairly quickly, and replaced by dollars and cents. Within as little as six months, it was quite unusual to see any shillings and pennies around. Sometimes a penny or a shilling still turned up here and there for years. So in 1967 all Australian school children had to learn the new *Metric System* using dollars and cents, which is easier because it uses the ten times table.

Even though Australians gave up their old money, they did not want to give up the Queen and her family! For example, the Hamilton Botanical Gardens has a statue of Queen Elizabeth's grandfather King George the Fifth. Also, in the 1960s, most classrooms, in Gray Street State School, had a photo of the queen on the wall. Queen Elizabeth the Second got the throne on Feb 6th 1952, after the death of her father, King George the Sixth. Everyone seemed very interested in the new queen. Even Australia's Prime Minister, Robert Menzies, admired her. During the queen's visit to Australia, in 1963, he said good things about Queen Elizabeth by repeating some famous words from a poem that was written for Queen Elizabeth *the First* (1533-1603), "I did but see her passing by and yet I love her till I die".

Everyone in Australia loved the queen and her family. A popular magazine, *The Australian Women's Weekly,* often had British information on its pages. A year after Queen Elizabeth became the queen, on 3rd June 1953, the magazine put a photo on its cover of a guard outside Buckingham Palace. The magazine celebrated the queen's first visit to Australia, in 1954, by showing her

the cover of The Australian Women's Weekly, February 1954

the 3 June 1953 of The Australian Women's Weekly cover showing a royal guard

on the front cover. She was smiling and happy with her husband, Prince Philip, on Sydney Harbour. Over time she showed that real beauty, that never fades, is a good character!

Most magazines were in boring black and white, because colour cost too much money. They only used colour for the front cover. But, when the queen came to Australia, the women's magazines also used colour *inside* their magazines, showing the queen's lovely dresses, hats, bags and shoes. Everybody, especially the ladies, wanted to see what the Queen was wearing!

Also, the people of Hamilton felt special when the Queen and her husband, the Duke of Edinburgh, visited them on February 26, 1954. One family, in Ballarat, even made a big crown in the front yard to show how much they loved the queen! Sadly for them the Queen did not visit Ballarat. Even though a lot of country towns invited her, only Mt Gambier and Hamilton were chosen, so people from other towns in Western Victoria felt very disappointed!

a crown in a front yard in Ballarat

[photo supplied by Helen Jenkin]

Nurses on the balcony of Hamilton Hospital greeting the Queen and waving flags

Hamilton rocked in Royal salute [1954, February 27]. The Argus [Melbourne, Vic. 1848 - 1956], p. 7. http://nla.gov.au/nla.news-article26593444

Hamilton residents wait for the Queen's car. Most women are wearing hats, gloves and coats, while the men are dressed in hats, ties and suits [photo supplied by Helen Jenkin]

The men have removed their hats as a mark of respect for the Queen as her car passes by.

[photo supplied by Helen Jenkin]

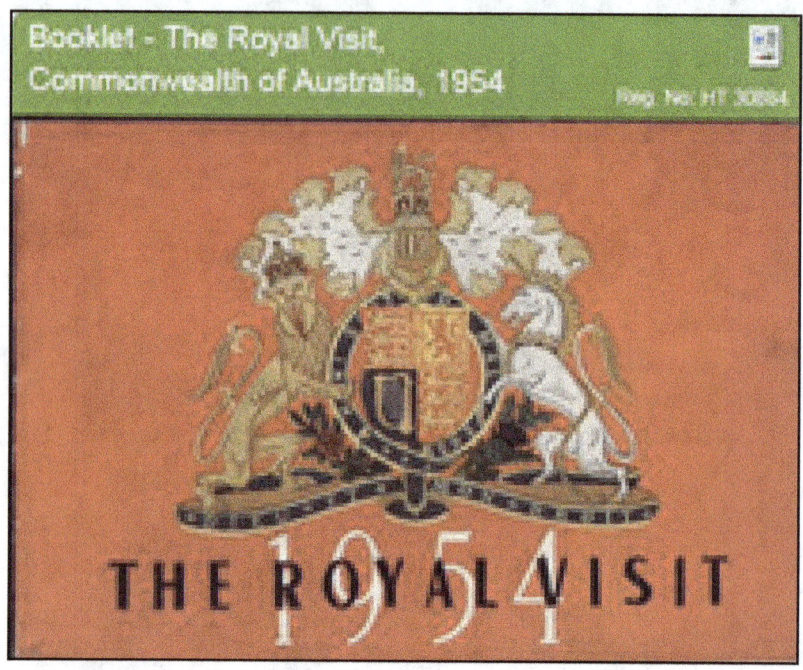

The Commonwealth Government gave out these booklets to schoolchildren in 1954, as a souvenir of the Royal visit by Queen Elizabeth II and her husband, the Duke of Edinburgh. The cover shows the British Coat of Arms.

1954 http://museumvictoria.com.au/collections/items/1821428/booklet-the-royal-visit-commonwealth-of-australia-1954

Hamilton celebrated the queen's visit. People decorated their windows with pictures of the queen and they also used paper, in the colours of the English flag: red, white and blue. There were English flags everywhere! When the Queen and her husband, the Duke, arrived at Hamilton Airport at 4 o'clock, they were welcomed by about 1000 happy local people. The couple were met by the mayor and his wife and then driven down Gray Street and Lonsdale Street to Melville Oval.

At the oval, about 13,000 school children had been waiting since 8.00am! These children were from 175 different schools and were standing in groups behind ropes. They didn't wear hats to protect themselves from the hot sun, and some fainted in the heat and were taken to sick bay!

It was lucky that some mothers had made extra sandwiches, and brought along some fruit, cool drinks and ice-creams for the children. Together with the children were several thousand other visitors. Many of them had travelled from far away to see the Queen. The *Canberra Times* newspaper reported that 50,000 people were there, which is a lot, because the people who lived in Hamilton were about 11,000! After the queen and her husband were driven round the oval, between the lines of cheering and happy children, a little girl gave a bunch of flowers to the Queen. Then the couple were driven along Foster and Bree Streets to the airport, for their plane flight to Melbourne.

When the queen returned to Australia for her second visit in 1963, she was again greeted by many cheering

In 1957 gloves and hats were a normal part of dress.

Theo is holding his godchild, Peter, and Argyro has Voula. [early 1957]

The Queen is accompanied by the Australian Prime Minister, Mr. Menzies, on March 10, 1954. He looks happy!

people. Argyro bought a lot of *Australian Women's Weeklies,* because she loved the many colourful photos of the queen wearing gloves, hats and often holding a matching handbag. Here is a part of the poem that Prime Minister Menzies said to show his respect and love of the Queen. It is in pink writing.

The poem was written by Thomas Ford [born 1580 – died 1648] who was an English musician and poet.

There is a lady sweet and kind,
There never was a face that so pleased my mind;
I did only see her passing by,
And yet I will love her till I die.</center> (1482 words)

https://en.wikipedia.org/wiki/Thomas_Ford_

Chapter 8
ANZAC Day

It was April 25th, ANZAC Day. Argyro and Theo were waiting together with other people outside Lucas Cafe. They were all waiting to watch the returned World War 1 and World War 2 soldiers, march along the main street. They were called Diggers. They marched wearing their ribbons and medals on their chests. As the soldiers marched in the Anzac Day Parade, their children often marched proudly beside them. It is still an Australian tradition and they still march in Hamilton to this very day. (You can check on the Internet for the Anzac Day notice in Hamilton, and the times of the different events.)

In the 1960s the returned soldiers got together at the corner of Kennedy and Gray Streets at 9:45am. It was always the same every year. Then, at 10 am they would start marching, led by a brass band in full uniform. Some men, with Scottish bag pipes and drums, marched along with them too. They joined together with the Hamilton Brass band. Also, it was an important event and many people watched them marching. They wanted to clap for them and to show their respect for the returned soldiers.

As more families arrived to wait along the main street, everyone was getting excited. Peter, Voula, Jimmy and Andy Hadis' children, Peggy, Theo, Steven and John felt very interested in the ex-soldiers. Voula watched their

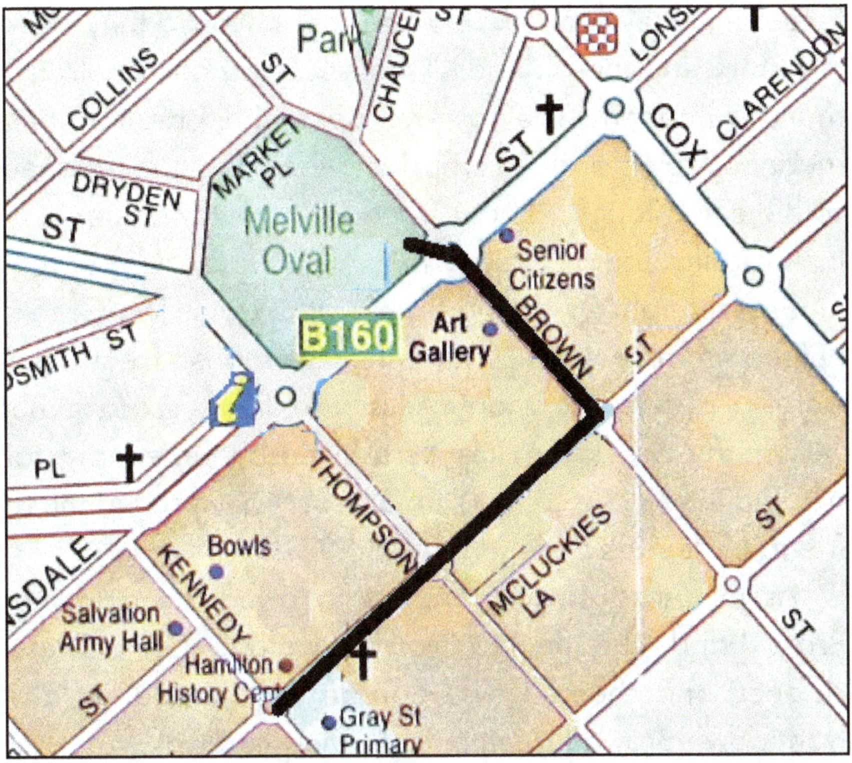

the marching route in black

Diggers marching in 1953

faces and they looked very serious, because they were remembering their friends, who had died and could not march with them. They always looked important in their medals! Argyro and Theo had told them that the returned soldiers had fought for our freedom and way of life, here in Australia and in Greece too. Australian soldiers were in Greece, fighting during both World Wars. The Greeks helped to hide them, from the Germans, when they were in danger, so many Aussie soldiers escaped. But very many Greek families were killed by the enemy, for helping the Aussie soldiers in Greece. They proved that a friend in need is a friend indeed!

As the Anzac Day marchers followed the Hamilton Brass band, the people watching along Gray Street, clapped and cheered. The parade then turned left and went down Brown Street towards Melville Oval.

When the returned soldiers arrived at the Melville Oval monument, the waiting crowd was asked to move away, so the marchers could enter the oval through the *Royal Australian Air Force* gates. Everyone was quiet, and even the cars stopped on the road. You could hear the marching shoes on the ground! The Hamilton *Returned Services League* (RSL) president always started the ceremony with a speech. His speech was like this:

"A time to be born, a time to die, ... a time for war and a time for peace."

Later, different groups of people, including school kids, put rings of flowers at the bottom of the monument,

a monument at Bonnie Doon, Vic.

to show their respect for the soldiers who died. Then, after singing a song, *Abide with Me*, the crowd sang *The National Anthem*. After that, the returned soldiers left, marching along Lonsdale St, and then finished for another year.

Near the monument were hundreds and hundreds of little white crosses, pushed into the grassy ground. Each cross was for a killed soldier, from Hamilton and nearby areas. The children were soon free to walk about and read the names on the crosses, as well as to look at the flowers placed at the monument.

In Australia there is another day to show respect for soldiers, *Remembrance Day*, also known as *Armistice Day* or *Poppy Day*, which is in November, on the 11th day. On this day, at 11 o'clock, there was complete silence in Gray Street State School. It started a couple of minutes before time, when the Head Master spoke over the speakers. Everyone had to stop what they were doing and think about the soldiers, who had given their lives for Australia's freedom. In Hamilton, even the cars on the streets stopped at 11am, while drivers showed their respect for the brave soldiers, who would never return home to their families.

On 11th November, in 1918, the Germans agreed for the fighting to stop, so they could talk together about peace, and their final surrender, to the *Allied Forces*. Later, paper poppy flowers were sold, and the money given to the war widows and their families. Red poppies were growing, where the soldiers were fighting, in Belgium and northern France, during the First World War. The soldiers said that the bright red colour of the poppies reminded them of the blood on the ground. So, the poppies are worn on *Remembrance Day*, each year. They help us remember that people died for our freedom.

These days *World War* soldiers are so few and weak, they are driven in cars, so they can be part of the Anzac Day Parade, along with younger, returned soldiers, from different wars. Of course Anzac Day is a public holiday, and people enjoy the break from work, and the chance to support all the returned soldiers from many countries, who march in the parade. (851 words)

red poppies growing wild

Today, Hamilton's Monivae College Band participates in the Anzac Day march. [used by permission of Monivae, Feb. 2016]

Voula, 6 years old, is kneeling beside Peter and Jimmy in front of the cenotaph. Her hair had grown back after being shaved off by Argyro. The Hadis boys are on her right. Notice the white crosses pinned into the grass, in the background.

the monument, Melville Oval, as it stands today

Chapter 9
Katie and The Beatles

Voula was very excited but tried not to show it. Her mother had told her that a teenage girl was coming to her house for a visit! One of Argyro's friends had a 14-year-old daughter, Katie, who was just crazy about *The Beatles* music band. *The Beatles* played *pop* music. The problem was that Katie didn't have a TV, but she really wanted to watch *The Beatles* concert. It was going to be in Melbourne and shown live all around Australia on the telly. "Your daughter is welcome," Argyro had told her friend, "Katie can visit and watch on our new TV." The television also had a radio next to it, with push-buttons, and above it there was a record player. It was a brand new style, a 3-in-1 unit, and the family was very proud of it!

This visit by Katie was a bit scary for Voula, because, up till now, her mother had only ever had Greek guests in her home. Argyro had always felt that British Australians would not respect her, as she couldn't speak English well and, so, she had never invited Australians into her home. Also, Voula and her brothers were not allowed to go on school camps, or on sleepovers to their friends' houses. Argyro thought other children might tease her children, or that her kids might learn bad ideas from the Aussie culture.

the 3-in-one, state-of-the-art entertainment unit

the Healing manual

the record player

the radio with its push-buttons and the top panel lifted to access the record player

Today Argyro asked Voula to make Katie feel welcome, but what could Voula do? She didn't have any experience! After thinking and thinking, Voula went to the mirror and practised her smiling. She looked at her open smile, showing her teeth and at her closed mouth smile. Which was better?

Well it was Wednesday, July 1st 1964, and Katie knocked on the front door. Voula opened it and said hello in a shy voice, but really she was happy, because it was great to have a "grown-up Australian" girl in her home! Voula took Kate into the lounge room and Katie sat on a sofa in front of the TV. Voula turned it on for her. "How do you change the station?" asked Katie. She asked this as she wanted to check the channels, because she wasn't sure which channel *The Beatles* would be on. Katie thought it might be HSV Channel 7, so Voula turned the dial to seven. They sat there watching the screen and waiting for the show to start.

After a quarter of an hour had past, and there was still no *Beatles* show, Katie got upset! She forgot her polite manners and left the sofa to sit on the floor, right in front of the television. She started changing the channels. Finally she found *The Beatles* band playing on channel 9, and was angry that she had not seen the very start of the show. Katie's eyes were glued to the telly. Voula sat with Katie and talked to her. She tried to make Katie feel welcome and at home. But Katie didn't listen to her. To tell you the truth, seven and a half-year-old Voula was not interested in *The Beatles*. Voula was secretly watching

Katie, not the TV.

Consequently, after a few minutes Voula saw something very sad: Katie was crying! Voula felt sorry for her and said to Katie, "Oh, Katie, don't be sad." Katie did not reply! Oh dear! Voula didn't know what to do. She felt uncomfortable and that she had not done a good job making Katie feel welcome in her home. Voula slowly began to move away from Katie until she was off the floor and sitting on the sofa, away from Katie. What should she do now? After a few more difficult minutes of quiet, Voula got up and walked into the kitchen to find her mother. "Katie doesn't want to talk to me! I don't know *what* to say and I don't want to be with her anymore." Argyro put some pressure on Voula, and replied, "You must stay with her. It's rude to leave her alone. I don't know *how* to speak with her." Argyro's English had grown slowly. She sometimes asked Voula to read letters that came in the mail box and tell her their meanings. Voula hated trying to explain the letters. She often didn't get the meanings. It was very difficult for her and it needed a lot of patience, that she didn't have.

Voula stood at the door of the lounge room and looked at Katie, who was smiling and crying at the same time! "Why are you crying Katie?" Voula asked quietly. Katie made a small try to chat a little with Voula, "Because I love *The Beatles* so much. I just love them! I wish I was one of the people in the audience. My favourite *Beatle* is Ringo Starr. Who is your favourite?" Unluckily, Voula did not even know *The Beatles'* names: John Lennon, Paul McCartney, George Harrison and Ringo Starr. She didn't know that their song, "Love Me Do" of December 1962, had gone to the top of the music world. Not only that, but *The Beatles* had started a new, long hairstyle fashion for the young, called the "mop-top". Voula answered Katie, "I like them all the same. They're all pretty good." Katie looked at Voula a bit uncertainly, not believing the little girl. It is well-known, that if you ask no questions, you'll hear no lies, for answers. After that Katie didn't speak to Voula any more! She watched the TV show very carefully, so she would not miss anything. She was dancing to the music too. Katie was trying to have a great time. She did not want to make *small talk* with a little seven-year-old girl: *The Beatles* show would be over too soon!

When the show ended, Katie turned off the television. Voula, was very surprised, because she thought Katie would ask her how to turn it off. Then Katie went into the kitchen to thank Argyro. After that she left quickly, and Voula didn't see her again! The experience with Katie had been very strange for Voula. She had looked forward to Katie's visit, but it had not gone well, because Katie did not seem friendly. Voula decided that teenagers were not normal. She did not want to become a teenager! Anyway her future seemed a very long time away for her.

About 45,000 Australians saw *The Beatles* six shows. The last show was taped for television by Channel 9 and shown in Australia on 1st July from 7:30 to 8:30pm.

Several days later, *The Beatles* were invited to the Melbourne Town Hall. All the important people came to welcome *The Beatles* to the city. *The Sun* newspaper reporter, Keith Dunstan wrote:

"At first, there was a hush and respectful clapping. Suddenly it *was on*. All around, girls were screaming, pushing forward, trying to stroke The Beatles' jackets. Young ladies, who five minutes before, had looked very correct, were screaming: 'WE LOVE YOU BEATLES'."
<www.onlymelbourne.com.au/the beatles-melbourne>

When parents listened to the news on the radio they heard that their teenage children were very badly behaved for pushing and screaming. Another thing people saw was *The Beatles'* long hair and they did not like it! But they could not stop their sons from copying their *mop-top hairstyles!* (1210 words)

The Beatles with their mop-top hair styles

from left: George, John, Ringo and Paul

In 1964 Voula was in grade 2B comprising 40 pupils! She is in the second row behind the girl holding the blackboard.

Chapter 10
Music

Trams, traffic lights and so many cars on the roads in Melbourne! Voula looked up, out of the bus window. There were so many electric wires for the trams! How was it possible to make so many power lines for all the trams? Where she lived, Hamilton, there was not even one traffic light. There were no trams, no wide roads and no large shops. Voula wished Hamilton did have these things because it would be a more important place. She continued to look at the big city sights with admiration as the bus travelled towards the Prahran hall. Her school recorder-band was going to play in a big musical competition. Every year many Victorian schools tried to win prizes at this competition. Gray Street State School usually did quite well.

It had all started for Voula in 1965 when she was in grade 3 and the music teacher, Mr. Sullivan, had taught every child from grades 3 to 6 to play the recorder. Argyro paid for Voula to buy her own recorder from Mr. Sullivan. It was made of wood and was a lovely light walnut colour. The school children who joined the school Recorder Band had to practise together twice weekly, at lunchtime. By the time Voula was in grade 5, Mr. Sullivan had asked her to play the treble, which was a larger recorder and she had to learn different positions for her fingers to make the

musical instruments from top left in order of mention

sounds. This recorder was made of beautiful rosewood.

To help the children to learn new songs, Mr. Sullivan wrote the music on large paper. He also helped them read the music by writing the letters above the notes. In this way he could easily teach all the children, of different ages, in the school Recorder Band. He used different colours for the music of the different musical instruments. He was a talented and enthusiastic musician. He was able to make all the instruments sound lovely together. There were different types of recorders, as well as drums, triangles, cymbals, maracas and even a horn. The horn was squeezed as the last sound, when a boy walked onto the stage in front of the band, to surprise everyone.

That year the school band won a prize in the Prahran competition and even made a small 7 inch record. Voula bought it as a souvenir of the recorder band's success. She felt very proud of

a 7" record

her school band. Maybe one day, they would become famous, like *The Beatles!*

Each year the band took the four and a half-hour drive to Melbourne. It took a bit longer than a car, because there were several stops for toilet breaks. First, the kids, teachers and some parents who were helping, were driven to a local primary school in Prahran. Here they were welcomed by the headmaster and pupils and given something to eat. After that, their names were called out, and they were introduced to some school children and their parents. Then they drove the Hamilton kids to their homes, where they were going to sleep for two days. To help the visitors not to be homesick, two or three Gray Street girls or two or three boys, stayed together with a family who had children of similar ages.

They only spent a little time in the homes, because after breakfast, they went to school with their host kids. During school times the Recorder Band was busy with activities and practising their music for the competition. When the school day was over, the parents took the children home for tea, supper and bed.

During the competition, the children had to wait their turn to perform. They were not allowed to speak during a performance and learned to clap at the right times. They were polite and clapped their hands for a competitor; even for or a bad performance. They were told about good behaviour and doing the "right thing". Often it took hours before their school name was called out, so each year they entered the competition, Voula knew she would get bored. Young kids don't have much patience and Voula was no different, although she did her best to enjoy the experience!

The next year, it was the turn of the Gray Street State School families to host the children from Prahran. Voula shared her bedroom with two little girls from Melbourne. They were very shy and it was difficult for Voula to know what to do with them until it was bedtime. She took them for walks to show them the neighbourhood, showed them her stamp collection and shared her game called *Spirograph*. It was a drawing game. It was a bit of a relief when they left after two days, because Voula was only nine years old, shy and had little confidence. At the end of 1968, Mr. Sullivan told the school he was leaving Hamilton. Sadly the Recorder Band ended. It had been a wonderful time for Voula and she kept playing her recorders into adulthood.

Not only did the school have a Recorder Band, they also had a choir of grade 3 to 6 pupils. When Voula was in grade 3, the choir teacher, Mrs. Criton, was looking for kids to sing in the choir, and asked children to come and stand by her piano one at a time. She tested their singing by playing a note on the piano, and asking them to sing it. Voula was able to sing the right note and was invited to join up, so she did. When Peter was invited to try-out the following year, he refused. He said the choir was for

Spirograph patterns

"sissies". Oh well, singing isn't for everyone!

In 1968, the school choir travelled by bus to Ballarat, a two and a half hour-long trip from Hamilton. They went there to appear on the local television station, BTV Channel 6. Ballarat held an annual Talent Quest at the Memorial Theatre, and the choir had been invited to sing on television, because they won third prize in Ballarat on 12 September 1968. In Ballarat there are still musical and singing competitions. The TV performance was not part of any competition, but just for entertainment. Voula was in grade 6 and felt excited about being on TV. The kids stood in 4 rows behind each other, on wooden boards and waited under the hot television lights. There were two cameras that rolled on wheels. There was a man behind each camera who controlled it. When the camera was working, the red light on top of it went on. Voula started perspiring with the heat, but tried hard to look relaxed as the camera moved across the faces of the singers. Still she couldn't help feeling very shy. However, things got worse when she got home.

It happened like this. One day, soon after returning from BTV Channel 6, Voula was walking home along Byron Street. One of the "big boys" who lived on the corner, at the bottom of Billy Goat Hill, was walking towards her on the footpath. Voula had always been afraid of the four teenage boys who lived in this house and played loud music and the drums. They seemed "wild" and she thought they did not obey their parents. In fact only two of the four were brothers, while the others were always visiting, because they had made a band and practised their music together: maybe they dreamed of being like *The Beatles*. It's interesting how a person's ideas are coloured by what they see, although not knowing all the facts! Argyro had warned Voula to keep away from these teenage boys, but now one of them walked towards her, on his way home. As they got closer to each other, she was amazed when he gave her a big smile. She automatically smiled back. Then he quickly changed his face to make it look angry and she quickly lost her smile too! Then he smiled again and she smiled too. This was strange! She tried to stop herself and not be like a puppet that he played with! Next time he smiled she didn't smile back. When they got close he made fun of her by saying, "Now we have a TV star in the neighbourhood!" Voula was surprised. She didn't know what to say. Although she felt scared, she kept walking, and did not run away. Her heart was beating fast! She felt thankful that he hadn't hit her or followed her. She held her breath, as there was still time for him to change his mind and tease her again. As the distance between them increased, she began to feel safer: it seemed he was pleased with his few words, and had left her alone! After that, whenever she had to go down Billy Goat Hill and past his house, Voula walked on the other side of the road. She even checked to see if anyone was coming up the road. It seems that being famous may bring quick glory, but it also brings shame too!

Argyro had asked Voula a question when she was nine years old, "Do you want to learn ballet or would you prefer piano lessons?" Voula loved the look of ballerinas in their special dresses as they gracefully jumped and turned on their tiptoes. Her bedroom curtains had lovely pictures of ballerinas. So, after a few days of thinking, Argyro was very surprised to hear her daughter's decision, "Piano!" The truth was that Voula thought she would probably lose interest in ballet, but to play piano would be useful all her life. Argyro spoke with Theo and they shared their ideas with his business partner, Andy, and asked for his advice. They soon learned there was an experienced music teacher, Mrs. Hughs, a widow right across the road from the primary school, in Kennedy Street. They decided that, to begin with, both Peggy, Andy's daughter, and Voula would share one half hour music lesson. This would help the parents to see how interested their daughters really were and save some money at the same time.

When the girls arrived at the teacher's house, Mrs. Hughs got one of them to copy some music on paper, whilst she gave the other girl a 15 minute piano lesson; then they swapped. Mrs. Hughs had very proper British ideas of behaviour, and because the girls were not her guests, but paying students, they were not allowed to ring the front door-bell. They were told to use the "trades" door on the side of the house. When inside, Voula noticed they were in a large dark room with several pianos and some covered tables and old furniture everywhere. The music teacher also knew how to do French Polishing and sometimes the room smelled of oil and alcohol.

Mrs. Hughs was a senior lady, but that didn't stop her from getting on the roof and fixing roof tiles. She must have been very fit! To Peggy and Voula, she was very strict and respectable, so they were always on their best behaviour.

Once, Mrs. Hughes told Voula that her husband had been a mayor of Hamilton and that she had been the first woman to graduate as an engineer from Melbourne University. Also, she was in the middle of writing a book about her family history, called Sleepers Two by Two. A couple of times Mrs. Hughs asked the girls to increase their lesson times, as their skills grew, so they did that, but the sharing of lessons continued for nearly three years.

Unfortunately the girls were too lazy, so they didn't practise much from one week to the next. Theo had taken his daughter to a music store, to choose a piano. Voula kept it in her bedroom. He encouraged Voula to do well in her musical skills, and Argyro nagged Voula to practise. However, Voula's learning was slow, because, although you can take a horse to water, you can't make it drink! After each lesson, when it was clear she hadn't practised playing her piano, Voula felt bad and decided to practise, but she didn't have the strength of mind to succeed. Both Voula and Peggy finished their music exams to grade 3 level, mainly because of the very patient Mrs. Hughs. Then the lessons came to a sudden stop at the end of primary school. (2061 words)

Argyro liked to dress Voula like a young lady. She is eight and a half years old and it is 29th June 1965.

the piano in Voula's bedroom & the "trades" entrance on the right used by the girls as they were not guests

Chapter 11
The Accident

It was the September holidays! In 1964, there were only *three* long, tiring school terms, not four like now; so the teachers and children really needed the holidays for a rest! Voula was nearly eight years old, her brother Peter was six and a half and Jimmy was almost four.

When Argyro worked in the cafe, helping during the busy lunchtime hours, the three children went to Lucas Cafe too. There was a little "private room," between the kitchen and the customers' dining area. There the children were allowed to play quiet games, as they tried not to feel bored. They liked to read or to colour-in the cartoons in the old black and white newspapers. Take-away fish and chips were put in newspaper in those days, and there was always a lot of papers in the private room. The newsagency next-door to Lucas Cafe, had lots of out-of-date newspapers they gave Andy. Also, every Thursday, new children's comic books arrived at the newsagency, so for this reason, Jimmy, Peter and Voula looked forward to Thursdays. Voula always took her time looking at the new comic books, smelling the new pages and deciding which one to buy. They usually bought comic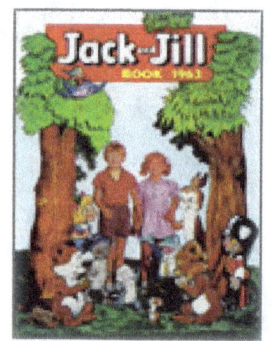

only half of the comic strip is shown
http://keaneoncomics.tumblr.com/post/15759618788/best-comic-strip-ever-scanned-from-the-romita

chips wrapped in newspaper

The children are at the Hamilton Baths during their September holidays.

The siblings are outside the newsagency and Jimmy and Peter are holding new comic book.

Used by permission: source world comics UK

Lucas Cafe, looking from the back "private room" of the shop towards the front door

books about *Jack and Jill*, *Superman*, *Tarzan*, *Super Heroes*, or *Richie Rich*. Today was just a normal day in the private room and they soon got bored. Jimmy didn't want to colour-in any more pictures in the comic strips. The kids were sick of being indoors. They wanted to get outside. Maybe they could go to Coles to buy some *Dairy Queen* ice-cream cones.

Since it was a beautiful spring day, Argyro let her children go to Woolworths and look for little toys to buy, like marbles or a small plastic car. Woolworths was closer than Coles, because it was only four shops away, down Gray Street. They would not be crossing any streets. If the kids left from the back door of Lucas Cafe, Woolworths was on the corner, the first shop around from the back street of the cafe. "Woolies" was a variety store in those days and it didn't sell much food. Customers looked at things on the counters. Lady shop attendants, behind the counters, helped customers and customers paid them. The ladies put items in a paper bag because no plastic bags were used in those days.

Argyro told her kids that because the cafe was very busy during that time of the day, they had to go out the back of the shop, so they wouldn't get in the way of the customers. Andy had told Theo it was bad for business, because it didn't look good if customers saw a bunch

 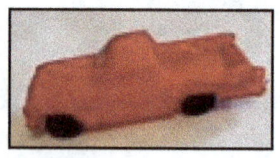 

a thru'pence, plastic car and some marbles

The three children walked past the old toilet, the wood pile and into the lane at the back of the shop.

inside Woolworths were counters with shop assistants waiting to serve customers

The street, McLuckies Lane, at the back of Lucas Cafe. The Woolies buiding is the red brick one on the front left. (picture taken 2014)

of messy children inside the shop. Therefore, the kids didn't go through the crowded shop full of lunch-time customers. They left through the back door with orders to hold Jimmy's hands and to take good care of him. The kids had a threepence coin with them, in Pete's pocket. They went out the back door, past the old toilet, past the wood used for the fire oven and into the quiet lane. It was used by all the shop owners, to park their cars or to get delivery of things for their shops. At the end of the lane they turned right into Thompson Street. They had only walked a few steps when they heard a cheeky, high voice calling, "Jimmy come and play with me!" It was Jimmy's kindergarten friend, Chris, a little Greek boy and a family friend. His family owned a cafe near where he was standing. He was laughing and waving his hand from across busy Thompson Street. Voula opened her mouth, to tell Jimmy he could not go across the road, but she felt his hand suddenly pull out of hers. "Oh no! Why didn't I hold him more tightly?" Voula scolded herself.

Then everything happened so fast, that it felt very strange. The traffic stopped. Voula saw people running onto Thompson Street. Suddenly she realised Jimmy had been hit by a car: actually a white utility! The driver got out and was bending over Jimmy's small body on the road! Voula turned away. Maybe if she didn't look she could pretend it did not happen. It could not be real! Voula was sure she was asleep and this was a bad, bad dream! Jimmy would be okay. He *had* to be okay! The shocked driver carried Jimmy to a lady, who was kneeling on the footpath. Jimmy's head was bleeding on her clothes. Maybe Jimmy wasn't hurt very much. Voula didn't want to look at her poor little brother, so she turned her head and looked at the "bad" driver who had hurt her brother. He looked like a farmer. He was wearing a big hat and a jacket. At that moment Voula thought of him as her enemy, because he had run over Jimmy. The farmer was looking down at the lady on the footpath and at Jimmy who was unconscious. The lady looked upset, and was asking the people around her if anyone knew the boy's parents. Voula thought, "Why isn't my mother here instead of this kind stranger?" Suddenly Voula wanted to help her brother and she found her voice. "He's my brother," Voula told her. The lady looked up at Voula and asked, "Where are your parents?" Then Voula understood she had something important to do. She replied to the lady, "I'll get them!" She turned to run past Peter who was crying. She ran back into the lane, trying with all her strength to return quickly to the cafe, to her parents, to get help.

However, something was very wrong. Her legs felt very heavy and they didn't want to move! Voula felt like her legs were trying to run in water. She again thought she was asleep, and this was a nightmare! For a moment she believed nothing was real! Then she remembered she had to find her parents. She thought she was wasting a lot of time: it might be faster if she tried walking, so she tried that, but it felt too slow. Voula was crying because she couldn't run fast. She started thinking about what she would tell her parents about Jimmy, and of the pain they would feel. She didn't want to tell them such bad news.

With a shock she realised she was still in the lane! It seemed to be taking forever to reach the back door of the cafe! Why couldn't she move faster at this time, when she really needed to? It was so important to be quick and she could not move fast enough!

Trying hard to make her heavy legs move, Voula finally reached the back door of the shop. It seemed to have taken a very long time, but at last she could tell her parents: they would know what to do. She felt wrong for not looking after her brother properly. Would her parents blame her? Was Jimmy badly hurt? Was he still alive?

Voula ran into the kitchen where the first person she saw was her Uncle George, grilling steaks for lunches. She told him quickly, "Jimmy's been run over by a car!" Voula could not believe that he laughed at her! She stared at him. She had not thought that he would not believe her. He thought she was playing a game! How could he think she would joke about something like this?! Her face changed, with fear and worry, and she squeezed her hands together, as she tried again to make her uncle believe her.

All of a sudden Voula turned around and came face-to-face with her mother, who had just come into the kitchen with some dirty plates for the sink. Voula was crying and her voice hurt her as she cried out, "Mum, Jimmy's been run over by a car!"

Her mother behaved completely differently from Uncle George. Argyro forgot everything! She dropped the plates she was holding. They crashed and broke on the concrete floor. "Yes, yes, it's true mum," Voula repeated scared that her Mama might not believe her after all. "Where is Jimmy?" demanded Argyro. Voula did her best to explain where she had left her little brother. Argyro ran through the shop to get Theo, and together they left to find their younger son. Everyone in the shop was talking about this sad news, as the customers realised something was wrong. Some of them ran out to see if they could help. Andy rang for the ambulance.

After some time, Voula realised Peter had come into the private room and together they waited there, through the afternoon. They were afraid and worried. They argued and blamed each other for not holding onto Jimmy's hands more tightly. They were having a horrible, bad time! Neither of them wanted to be blamed for the accident, and attacking someone else is the best way to defend yourself! They were scared stiff! They waited hours for their parents to return, but they were scared about what would happen next. It seemed so *unreal*. How was it possible that the world could continue on, as if nothing had happened to take away their peace?! (1540 words)

Here is the brick wall of Woolworths, where the children were when Chris called out to Jimmy from across the road. You can see the lane on the right side.

A 1950's ute ran over Jimmy.

Chapter 12
Celebrations

Two nights later Voula was in bed trying to sleep when she heard her mum's footsteps as she entered her bedroom. "Are you asleep?" Voula heard her mother ask. Voula felt her bed move when her mum sat on the bed. She knew her mother had just returned from the hospital. "Will Jimmy be alright?" she asked, but she was afraid of her mum's answer. Her mother spoke with sadness, "Jimmy has lost a lot of blood. Also he needs to have some skin taken from his thigh and put onto his chest. His left leg is broken and some ribs too. Please pray for him Voula, because God loves children. Maybe God will hear your prayers and help Jimmy to get better." Argyro and Voula cried together, and Voula could not get rid of the lump in her throat. She felt better that her mother didn't blame her, or Peter, for Jimmy's accident. Her mum was not angry: but she looked sad and very tired. Argyro could not sleep well. Anyway, sleep cannot help when your soul is tired.

Voula thought, "No one can help Jimmy: only God. He is fighting for his life!" That was the first time Voula really prayed to God; it was personal. She cried as she prayed, and her tears felt hot as they ran down her cheeks. She felt like her world had broken, and that life could never be the same again! Would God really save Jimmy? Voula

Jimmy with his leg in plaster, is standing at the back door of the house.

prayed again, and as often as she remembered. She made a deal with God, that if God saved Jimmy, then she would believe He was real.

Luckily, time often heals and happily, Jimmy slowly got better and was sent home with plaster on his leg. Theo carried Jimmy into the house and Voula knew God had given her little brother another chance at life, so she remembered to thank HIM. Her heart offered a song of joy as she realised that God was *good* and *real* and had answered *her* prayers.

The family was overjoyed to have Jimmy back again and Argyro tended to his every little want. He was her special child because she had nearly lost him. Nothing was too much for Jimmy! Unbelievably soon, life became normal again, except that Jimmy couldn't move very fast, or very far, for a few more months. When Jimmy's fourth birthday in October got close, Theo rang the Hamilton newspaper, *The Spectator*. He asked if they would like to come to his house, to take a photo of Jimmy on his birthday. They agreed to send a reporter to write a story about the little boy, who was getting better, after the terrible accident of a few weeks ago. The newspaper would also send a photographer to take a picture for the newspaper. Counting down the days until the birthday, the family became very excited.

On the day of the party some of the neighbourhood kids and friends were invited. They all wore party hats, blew up balloons, ate lots of food and had too many lollies. Since Voula's birthday was only nine days after Jimmy's, the party was for both Voula and Jimmy together.

the newspaper photo that appeared in The Spectator

from left: Niki (Chis's big sister), Alana who lived in the neighbourhood; Peter and his best friend Bob, Voula, Theo Hadis, Jimmy, Steven Hadis, Cousin Peter, Peggy and John Hadis

Voula wore a hat with stars on it for the newspaper photo, which was put on the front page. It shows Jimmy wearing a bow tie and no plaster on his leg. But the best things about the photo are the smiles on Theo's and Argyro's faces. Their son was alive and well!! Their hearts were very happy and they felt on top of the world!

School continued. Voula and her classmates in grade 2 played games together like: *Hidey, Kick the Tin, Skippy, Elastic* and *Hop Scotch*. The boys played football and cricket or fighting games. The children were separated, because the boys played on the oval and the girls played their games on the tarred area.

school games from left: Hidey, Kick the Tin, Hop Scotch, Skippy, Elastic

The shelter sheds had seats along the inside walls.

When it rained everyone ran into the *Shelter Sheds* to wait for the bell to ring, to go back into their classrooms. In the sheds they could use the seats along the walls to play the game of *Cat and Mouse*. The "Cat" stood in the middle of the shed and tried to catch the "Mice" as they ran along the seats, from their safe corner to another corner. When a "Mouse" was caught as it tried to run to a corner, it became the "Cat"!

Every year Gray Street Primary School, Hamilton 295, had a tradition. At the end of the year, on the last day, the whole school walked in their grades to the Prince Regent cinema, two blocks away. The children walked in pairs, holding hands and chatting, as they went down Gray Street. They walked past Lucas Café and turned right at the end of the block. When all the school was seated inside the cinema Mr. Harris, the headmaster, welcomed them and wished everyone a happy holiday over Christmas. Then everyone stood up to sing the National Anthem, *God Save the Queen*. After that, the lights went off and the movie began.

It was a lot of fun and very exciting. Usually, it was a comedy. At half time, after the first movie, the teachers gave each pupil an ice-cream to enjoy. Then the second movie would begin. Of course, in those days there was no sex or violence in movies. The worst thing you could see was "Cowboys" shooting "Indians" or cowboys having a gunfight. There was never any blood.

Disneyland movies were very popular, and the school saw many Disney films over the years. Two of them were *Bambi*, and *Snow White and the Seven Dwarves*. After that,

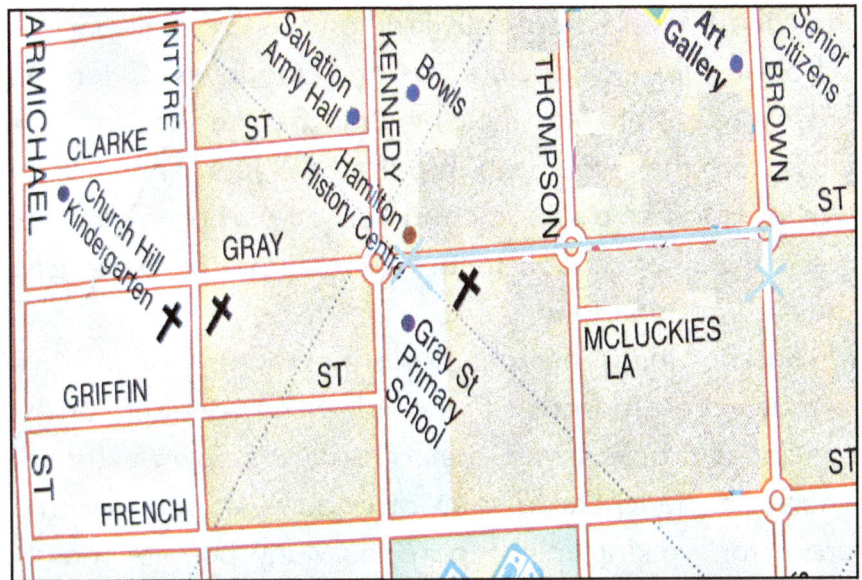

The blue line shows the path taken by the pupils to the cinema, which since then has been converted to shops, below.

The Prince Regent cinema has changed hands, but the original name is still visible under the curve of the roof.

the children were pleasantly tired and ready to go back to school for their class cleanups and goodbyes. Often the kids were sent to visit their new teacher and to sit in the classroom they would go into the next year. The change was as good as a holiday and was all part of the thrill of the last day of school, before it was time for home and the summer holidays!

Another thing the school did every year was to have a fancy dress parade. The children got dressed up as special characters and met outside the town's library. There, the teachers tried to arrange everyone in some order for walking in the parade. Many people, mainly parents, waited along Gray Street, to clap as the parade passed them. When the time came, a musical band started playing and led the parade as it walked down the street. The children came behind the band and the parents, cheering and clapping, joined in and followed the children, until everyone walked through the main gate into the school ground.

Then began the yearly school fete! The headmaster thanked everyone and announced the winner of the dress parade. It was a bit of an honour to win, so Voula felt lucky to win it the first year she wore her Greek National Costume, when she was in grade 4. Her mother had spent long hours making it. The jacket was of deep red velvet, and the skirt was of green silk. After that she wore the same costume, again and again, even when it became too small for her in grade six! Voula had asked her mum to make something else for her, but Argyro told Voula to wear her National Costume. "It's important Voula, to show

Voula in grade 4 with Peter in grade 3. They are standing beside the stump of the palm tree mentioned in Chapter 20. Bob's house is in the background.

In their National Greek Costumes walking in the parade, Jimmy looks a bit shy while Voula has outgrown hers.

people we are proud of our country." That's probably why both Jimmy and Peter also wore their home-made Greek National Costumes in the school parade year after year too. However, Voula never won a prize for her costume again, because everyone got used to seeing it every year!

At the school fete, pony rides were always popular. Also, there were mothers selling home-made cakes, biscuits and jams. There was a Merry-Go-Round and Fairy Floss. Also there were competitions to guess how many buttons or beans were in glass bottles, or to see who could throw a tennis ball the furthest.

A popular event was the *Sand Saucer Floral Competition*. The winners were decided by the Mothers Club. Children were invited to bring along a saucer of wet soil or sand and some flowers. The teachers gave them some time during school to put the flowers on the saucers. The many beautiful saucers of flowers were put in the school library. The best ones had ribbons on them for first, second and third prizes. Don't ask me how they were judged, because they were all beautiful!

All the classrooms were open, so parents could walk in and see their children's classwork on the walls, and look into their kids' desks. It was a good family time, and a time for the school to make some money, to buy things that the school needed. (1470 words)

looking inside an empty school desk

floral arrangements on little saucers of soil or sand

Peter G, dressed in his cowboy costume, awaits the start of the parade.

Chapter 13
Fun, Games and Pets

Often, migrant families share a house until they can save up a bit of money to rent or buy their own place. This is what happened when Theo's younger brother, George, arrived in Hamilton in February of 1961. George was married with a child, a son, Peter. Why did Theo have a son named Peter too? Well "Peter" had been the name of Theo's and George's father. This was their way of showing respect for their father, by continuing his name. That is what Greek people do. To make a difference between the two Peters, one was called Peter T after Theo, and the other Peter G, after George. As time passed, Peter T became just plain Peter, but for his cousin, the name Peter G stayed for his whole life! Cousin Peter G and his parents, lived with Argyro and Theo for three years, until they saved up enough money to buy their own house in Goldsmith Street, only a few houses away and down the hill from Peter's house. By the time both Peters were aged 6, they both liked the same things; both had strong personalities and both liked to have their own way.

Not many people in Australia had televisions before the middle of the 1960s, so what did the two Peters, and other children, do in a small town, to pass the time? Well they made up their own games! Peter for example, used to like playing with toy cars. One day his parents gave

 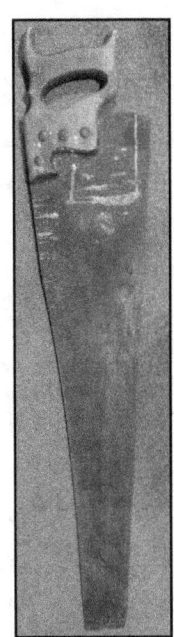

the old table in the garage and the rusty saw

him a tin fire-engine that was about 30 centimetres long. They also gave one, exactly the same, to Peter G. The two Peters spent many happy hours together making pretend roads in the dirt, for their fire-engines.

Anyway, one day, the two Peters were playing in the old garage, in the back yard. One of the fire-engines got damaged. No one was sure how it happened. Peter said that it was his cousin's fire-engine that was damaged. Of course Peter G said that his own fire-engine was the undamaged one. So they had a big fight and yelled at each other! They both lost their tempers! Both boys had very red faces, because they were so angry!

Suddenly, Peter took the undamaged truck and started to walk out of the old garage. Peter G did not want to let Peter take the better truck for himself. He wanted to do something to stop him. In the garage there was an old, rusty saw. Cousin Peter took the saw and banged it into the top of Peter's head! OUCH!! Peter at once let go of the truck he was holding, to touch his sore head and to feel his cuts. He could hear his head inside. It was banging like a drum! Lots of blood was coming out of his head onto his hair, over his face and down his neck and shoulders! He forgot about the firetruck. He ran into the house to find his mother to get help. Voula ran after him; she had seen the whole thing. The kids found Argyro in the kitchen cooking lunch for them, and humming a Greek song to herself.

Well! You can imagine the fear on poor Argyro's face! She cried out, "Aargh!" and then asked what had happened. At the same time, she looked in his hair, trying to find where the blood was coming from. On his head she saw a straight line of holes made by the teeth of the saw. Unluckily, they were quite deep and bleeding a lot! From the amount of blood, and because the saw was old and rusty, Argyro knew it was serious. It could become infected. She had to do something quickly!

Argyro couldn't drive and she didn't have a car. She called out from her kitchen window to her neighbour, Margaret Shmitz. When Margaret put her head out of her own window, Argyro called to her to ring for a taxi, to take them to the hospital. Next she pushed a clean tea towel onto Peter's head and held it there. Then they went outside to wait for the taxi, which arrived very quickly, as Hamilton is a smallish town. The doctor put ten stitches in

Peter's head, gave him an injection, and sent him home to rest!

Cousin Peter got a smack on his bottom and was told not to fight again! Peter had to stay inside for a few days with his mother watching him very carefully. The two Peters did some reading, played with their marbles or made armies with their little green plastic soldiers. Sometimes they laughed and sometimes they argued. Things were back to normal again. What do you expect? That's life, isn't it!?

Voula also had some bad experiences. One winter evening she was playing near the kitchen stove. It was an old, iron stove. On top it had flat, iron plates that were heated by the wood fire. Argyro put her cooking pots onto these plates to cook the family meals. There was also an oven underneath and right at the bottom were two long drawers. In these drawers Argyro put wet pieces of wood to dry, ready to go into the fire.

One evening, Voula opened the bottom drawer, so the family's kitten could get in and warm itself up. The kitten often liked to do that! Sadly, Voula forgot about the kitten and walked away. Someone closed the drawer without seeing the kitten still asleep inside. So the next day, when Argyro bent over to see if there was some dry wood in the drawer, she had a nasty surprise —a dead pussy cat! What could she do? It was too late to do anything! The poor little kitten was dead! But there were some other kittens in the garage and the kids soon made friends with them and felt sad for only a *short* time. After that, they did not let any cats warm up in the bottom drawer!

Mother Cat was always busy having kittens and caring for them. She had kittens twice or three times a year! The children learnt that there were other ways cats could die, even without being forgotten in an oven drawer. They learnt you shouldn't touch baby kittens, if they are too young to open their eyes! If the kids did touch newborn kittens, then the kittens would grow white milky stuff in their eyes. After that, sadly, they got very sick and died! The children had to be patient and wait for the kittens to grow, and to be able to use their eyes. Then the kittens would be strong enough to stay alive when the children played with them. However, sometimes the children found the kittens so cute, they couldn't stop themselves from holding them—for just a little while. If they did, then the kittens would die, even after being so greatly loved! It taught the kids self-control!

Well, Voula sure liked being close the stove on cold

Jimmy with a pint of milk, is feeding Mother Cat and two of her kittens.

some head stitches

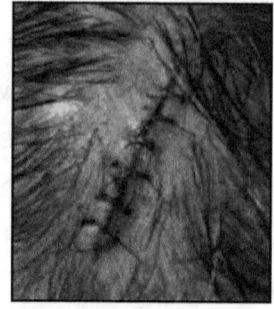

Peter G and his mum are with Voula, Peter and Jimmy.

The damaged fire-truck became Jimmy's favourite toy.

a wood fired stove and oven

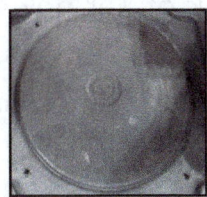

an iron hotplate

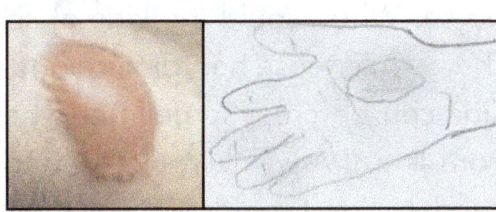

Voula's palm with its huge burn blister

The concrete laundry sinks are now in the garden.

a can of petrol

evenings, because it felt so warm and cosy to stand nearby. There was no other heating in the house, except for the open fire-place in the lounge room, which was not always lit. One time Voula was jumping up and down, next to the stove, when she suddenly tripped. To stop herself from falling, she put the palm of her hand on one of the hot iron plates, and pushed herself away from the stove. She saved her face and chest from being burned but her poor palm, just under her thumb, got burnt and felt very hot and sore. Her mother put it under cold water and then put butter on it. In those days everyone thought that was the thing to do. However, when Voula woke up the next morning she saw something that was horrible! A big bubble blister of skin had grown overnight! Not just a small bubble but a HUGE bubble! It was the size of a small egg! Also, it hurt!

Voula knew that her classmates would make fun of her if they saw her big blister. Kids don't want to be different from other kids. She was already different because her parents were migrants, but now it would be much, much worse! What would the kids at school think of her now? They would tease her for sure and call her unkind names. Kids can be cruel sometimes when someone is different from them! Anyway Voula tried to hide her blister with a Band-Aid, but it didn't cover much. The blister was easy to see. Voula kept her hand behind her back or hid it in her sleeve, or in a pocket. She got good at hiding it. Then, one day she fell over on the wet bathroom floor and the blister broke! It stopped hurting and felt so good after it broke! Voula wondered why she had not thought of breaking it herself! Her hand was normal again! What a relief!

Another time Argyro let Voula watch a TV show called *Combat*. It showed muddy soldiers shooting the enemy in World War 2. There was no blood, just dirty soldiers. The soldiers used petrol and poured it along the road to an enemy truck. Then they hid far away and threw a match on the petrol. Voula was amazed to see a line of fire run quickly to the truck and then....KABOOM! She thought about it for days. Then she decided to use some petrol that was used for the lawn mower. She undid the small cap of the petrol can, and poured some of the petrol into the cap. Where could she put it for safety? The two laundry sinks were made of concrete. She felt sure the concrete was strong enough to keep the fire that she planned to light with a match. Voula carefully put the cap of petrol in the bottom of a sink. Then she had trouble lighting a match, but finally she did it! She only had a second to hold the match in the air, about 30 centimeters from the cap, before she dropped the match in fear! The petrol had caught fire BEFORE she got the match near the cap of petrol! The petrol fumes had caught fire! The fire went up through the air, burning her front hair, eyelashes and eyebrows. That's why the petrol can said "highly flammable!"

Voula ran into the house to find her mother. Voula quickly explained what had happened and Argyro checked that there were no burns on her daughter. Then she smacked Voula on her bottom, for being naughty and playing with petrol and fire. Argyro told Voula to learn her lesson and not to do anything like that ever again!

However, not long after, Argyro *herself* decided to do something she was later sorry about. In the 1960s, people didn't think much about being kind to animals. Argyro had grown up on a village farm, and they used to kill animals for food. She was very practical about animals. Anyhow, Argyro got sick and tired of Mother Cat always having so many kittens. She decided to take away this cat! Argyro put Mother Cat in a box with her kittens, and because they didn't have a car, she asked Mr. Hadis to drive her to the country-side, outside Hamilton. There they put the box beside some trees and drove home. This was not unusual in those days and other people did this too.

Voula didn't know what her mother had done. She called for Mother Cat every day, to feed her, "Here puss, puss, puss!" but the cat did not come. Then one day Voula saw an old-looking cat in the back yard. It was very thin and Voula could see its bones under its fur. Voula got some milk in a saucer for the cat, but it did not trust her and it waited until Voula walked away. Then she watched through a window, as the cat went to the saucer to lick up the milk. Voula went to tell her mother, but the cat had gone when Argyro went to see it.

A few days later the cat returned, and this time Argyro saw it. With a shock she knew it was Mother Cat, who had found her way back home! Argyro felt very bad when she saw the poor cat! They say it is good for your soul to tell what you have done that is wrong. So Argyro told her kids what she had done. She promised never to do the wrong thing to their pets, ever again. Never again did Mother Cat come near people, and never again was Argyro unkind to an animal. Well, except for the hens who stopped laying new eggs, because they wanted to sit on their old eggs. The hens wanted to keep them warm and try to grow little chicks. To start these chooks laying eggs again, Argyro did something that she had learnt from her village life in Greece. It wasn't pleasant, but it always worked! (2178 words)

Theo with his brother George

Sitting on their swing are: Cousin Theo, Peter holding Mother Cat, Peter G holding Ginger and Jimmy holding a toy car.

Chapter 14
At Home

During the week the family did the usual things: the parents continued to work, Theo in the Café every weekday, and for half a day on Saturdays. Argyro tried to organise and clean her home. However, when it got busy in the café, Argyro went to help, as a waitress. She got very good at holding plates of food; she could hold three plates on each arm. It was amazing to see!

Since Argyro was so busy, Voula was often told to do the housework. Because she was a girl, Voula had to vacuum and to do up the beds. As Argyro often told Voula, all this housework would help her to become a good wife and mother one day. "It's not fair!" Voula often replied. Why did she have to do her brothers' beds? So, even though Voula wanted to be playing outside, she often had to help her mother: usually she complained a lot!

Argyro wanted to train her only daughter very well. Over the years, she carefully instructed Voula how to water the garden, vacuum the house, sew, knit, cook and bake. Voula's sultana cakes became popular in her family. Even Mrs. Hadis wanted her daughter, Peggy, to learn to make this sultana cake too. One day Voula visited Peggy, and Mrs. Hadis took the girls to her kitchen. She wanted to learn the recipe: high praise for a young girl. They used fresh eggs for the cake, because the Hadis family had

Voula is watering the front garden.

 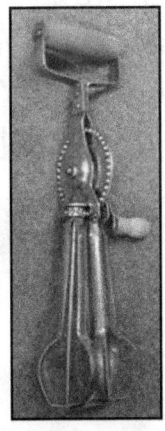

Argyro showed Voula how to use a flour sifter and an egg beater.

chooks. Voula was shocked one day when she arrived at Peggy's back gate. There, running around the back yard was a headless chook, chased by Mr. Hadis. It was the rooster that had been biting the hens. Now it was going to be the family's dinner! After that Voula didn't feel like eating chicken for a very long time.

One of Voula's jobs was to keep the house clean, but it was very hard to do because of the boys. Peter, and his best friend Bob, often took a quick way to the back yard by walking through the front door, through the passageway and out the back door! They could easily have walked to the back yard outside. But n-o-o-o *they* chose to walk *through* the house, wearing their muddy boots. The newly-vacuumed, crimson carpet was made dirty very soon! Aargh! Voula complained to the boys when they did this. She would run to the front door just in time to tell them to stop. They didn't obey her as *boys will be boys*. They didn't want her to think she could be their boss, so they walked through the house with their dirty shoes anyway.

This was how Voula got the reputation of being "bossy." You see she didn't give up trying to teach the boys that they shouldn't walk through the house with muddy shoes.

typical of those times: a ceramic kettle and a tin car

Argyro bought Voula her own sewing basket.

from left: Peter, Voula, Jimmy and Bob in the Botanical Gardens

Sometimes they felt sorry for her and held their boots in their hands, but Voula always felt it was because she had *nagged* them, and not because they had finally learnt some *common sense*!

However, it wasn't only Voula fighting with the boys and trying to get them to do the right thing. One day, Peter made his mother very angry! It happened because Peter liked *The Lone Ranger* on the telly. It was about a cowboy and his Indian friend who helped people in trouble. The *Lone Ranger* was a "goody" and Peter admired him a lot. He really loved the way the *Lone Ranger* could jump out of a high window, or from a balcony, to get on his horse! The *Lone Ranger* often whistled for his horse to come to him. Then he would jump onto his horse and quickly get away from the "baddies" who were trying to hurt him.

That morning Peter had left his bicycle under the kitchen window, which was about one and a half metres from the ground. After having his breakfast of scrambled eggs, he said goodbye to his mother. Quickly Peter climbed out of the window, just above his much loved bike. Argyro, was very surprised! What was Peter doing? She ordered him to get off the window and to come back inside. At that moment Argyro saw that Mrs. Margaret Shmitz, her neighbour, was looking out of *her* window. Argyro felt ashamed of what Margaret might be thinking.

Peter was feeling cheeky and he was having a lot of fun. He wanted to get onto his bike for a "quick getaway". Peter thought to himself, "This is just like the *Lone Ranger!*" Argyro was very upset when he didn't obey her. He looked like he wanted to continue with his fun. Argyro secretly thought it was funny, but she wanted Peter to obey her. She reached for the nearest thing she could throw at her son: it was a fresh egg! She threw it and it landed on top of Peter's head, just before he could ride away, "splat!" The egg left a sticky mess in his hair, that his mother had to help him wash out later. After that he was not allowed to make a "quick getaway" and only did it again when he thought his mother wouldn't see him!

The passage-way in 2010. You can see the front door; a runner has replaced the crimson carpet to show the beautiful, original timber floor.

the kitchen window looking from the street

looking out of the Argyro's kitchen window at Mrs. Shmitz's long kitchen window

the Lone Ranger with his horse, Silver

with his faithful side-kick, Tonto

As Argyro had studied dressmaking in Athens, so she could sew very well. She often made lovely clothes for her only daughter. Voula's dresses were full-skirted and often had lace. They were very girly. One of her favourite dresses was worn to Sunday School at the local *Church of Christ*. Because there were no *Greek Orthodox* churches in Hamilton, Argyro's kids went to Sunday School there. Anyway, her dress was pale pink with a wide belt tied in a bow at the back. By the time Voula got back from *Sunday School*, lunch was on the table, so she usually didn't change out of her nice clothes till later. Often, after lunch, she just wanted to keep wearing her favourite dress. To tell the truth, she was too lazy to change out of her best dress. This was a big mistake to make as we will see!

One Sunday she went outside in her lovely dress to play *Cowboys and Indians* with Jimmy and Peter. The boys told her that they would be the cowboys and Voula would be the Indian. They gave her a small plastic bow and some arrows to shoot. Then Peter told her they didn't have any *guns* to shoot her with, so they were going to "shoot" her with water, from the garden hose. Peter had turned on the water and was holding the water hose, ready to "shoot" her. "That's not fair!" said surprised Voula, as she ran to the water tap to turn it off. Peter told her to keep away from the tap or he would shoot water at her. Then he laughed at her and pointed the hose at her. She stopped and stood with her hands on her hips. She angrily told Peter, "You wouldn't *dare* wet me! I'm wearing my best dress!" The next thing she knew was that cold water was going through her dress and onto her skin! Voula yelled in anger, but Peter kept watering her like she was a dry flower needing water, until Voula ran away to tell her mother.

It was hard for Voula to understand what Argyro told her, "Don't play with boys. You should know better!" So, Voula was even more upset than ever! She felt the world was unfair to her!

Another example, of fun for the boys, was the time they played football in their bedroom. Often Peter and Jimmy fell on the walls, floor and beds with loud bumps. Sometimes the ball hit their bedroom window and broke it. Over time, they learnt to use "soft balls" because of the many times Argyro told them not to throw balls inside the house. They got the idea of practising their ball-kicking, by using a ball made of socks. As there were quite a few socks used to make the "ball", it was pretty heavy and when Peter kicked it to Jimmy on the other side of their bedroom, it sometimes hit the window and broke the glass again! (This window was actually broken several times.)

They say a woman's work is never done. Argyro had to vacuum her sons' room very carefully, again and again, to make sure no little pieces of glass would get into her sons' bare feet—there seemed to be millions of bits of glass everywhere! Also their beds had to be changed too, and the sheets shaken out. Argyro thought she had got it all out of the carpet, but for several weeks she kept finding broken glass in the boys' bedroom! When would the boys learn to be more careful? (1466 words)

the Church of Christ

a ball made of socks
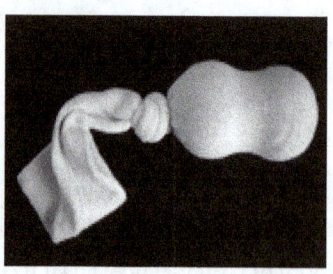

Theo with his children, Voula [hands with her hands on her hips], Jimmy and Peter in the back yard. Peter loved wearing his cowboy outfit and even held some corn his mum had grown.

Theo and his family are holding Greek-style Easter eggs: the red, hard-boiled ones. It is just seven months after Jimmy's accident on 25/4/1965.

Chapter 15
Obsessions and Hobbies

After Jimmy's accident, there were no more unlucky events, but Voula often worried about the accident. She tried to understand *why* it had happened. Why Jimmy? Why *her* family? All people think about *why me*, at some time in their lives. Why, why, *why* did bad things happen? Most times there is no answer to this common question about life. She asked her mother and Argyro replied that it had just been bad luck and that, sometimes, these things happened.

Voula started thinking about *good luck* and *bad luck*. Was there anything she could do to keep evil away, and to make sure good things happened? She began to take notice of other people's idea about luck like: if you blow out all your birthday candles, your wish will come true; never walk under a ladder, and her teacher said that some people thought that breaking a

After Jimmy's accident, Voula wanted to stop bad luck from happening to her family.

mirror, would bring seven years of bad luck. Then Voula realised she was not the only one to think about good and bad luck. Others had been thinking about this too! She was not alone. People had thoughtfully made some rules for her to follow!

On a certain day, as Voula, Peter and Jimmy were walking to school, Voula happened to notice a caterpillar on a tree by the side of the footpath. She stopped to look at it and walked around the tree for a better view. Then she hurried to catch up with her brothers. Suddenly a thought stopped Voula. Everything had been going well in her life since the accident, but what if changing her path from her regular walk to school, would bring bad luck? Was it good luck versus bad luck? Was it just lucky that everything was going well with her family or was it some special behaviour that brought good luck? What if her walk around the tree, which had been different from her usual path, made a different future? Would it bring bad luck? She ran back to the tree and circled around it to the side she would normally go past and then walked at a normal speed, back to her brothers.

Next, she noticed some other things like an uneven crack in the footpath and decided it would be bad luck to step on it. When she crossed the road, she decided to walk north and then turn west, not west first and then north. Coming home, she felt she had to walk on exactly the same path, to "undo" the walking she had done in the morning. Her

It was bad luck to step on a crack in a footpath!

fear of making bad luck for herself and her family grew. Voula became more careful about where she walked first, in her bedroom and second and third. Day after day, week after week, Voula followed strict walking patterns. She felt trapped, unable to get out of her fear of bad luck. She didn't know that there is a name for this type of mind behaviour: *Obsessive Compulsive Disorder* [OCD].

She was proud to be the eldest child and felt responsible to help her family. Not in a million years did she want her brothers to know what she was doing. Voula knew she was being a bit silly and felt ashamed to let anyone know about her behaviour, so she took care to walk behind Peter at the right places. She didn't want Peter to see and she hoped Jimmy was too young to notice. However, one day as they were walking home, Peter asked her, "Why do you always walk around that tree clockwise and then anticlockwise?" Voula replied, "I want to." Peter told her he thought she was doing stupid things. He had found out her secret! To show him, that he was wrong she stopped her special walking patterns. She even walked on the crack on the footpath!

The next few days Peter watched Voula carefully and Voula watched Peter too. If he was watching she didn't follow her plans to stop bad luck. After some time, she realised that nothing "bad" had happened and she was "cured". Sometimes she did follow her special walking patterns, but with time, she forgot about bad luck. It is not always as easy as that, for people who are *obsessive* about something, to stop behaving in a strange way.

In the 1960s, people often became obsessed with

a *hobby*. During their leisure time, some people would collect things like: coins, dolls, spoons and plates: anything really. Others just enjoyed a hobby for fun and were not obsessed! Argyro, had siblings in Greece and received mail with Greek stamps on the envelopes. She used the stamps to educate Voula about Greece, Hellas. The stamps often showed the Greek royal family, the heroes from mythology and the ancient Greek gods.

Argyro showed her daughter how to remove the stamps by soaking them in cold water until they could be easily peeled off the envelope. Then they dried the stamps for a day and put them in her stamp album. Most stamp albums had names of countries on different blank pages where the collector would paste their stamps. However, Voula's album had open rows of clear plastic for the stamps to be placed into. The stamps could easily be rearranged and moved about, but there were no headings for the countries.

Argyro encouraged Voula to collect *used* stamps rather than buying packets of unused stamps from the post office. It was a slow process until Auntie Tasia from Greece heard that Voula was starting a stamp collection. Tasia was eleven years older than Voula and had just graduated as a secondary school teacher. She kindly sent Voula most of her stamps in her next letter to Australia. Voula started to eagerly organise her stamps. She was very seriously stuck on stamp collecting, for several months. She thought Auntie Tasia was her best auntie and must love her very much, to give up her own stamps to her niece like that! The Australian stamps she had were

part of Voula's stamp album: Greek stamps

Australian stamps

from bills and letters from Argyro's sister in Melbourne and a cousin from Adelaide. They were five cent stamps and the queen looked very young and beautiful.

Voula's favourite stamps, because of their unique shapes, were an Egyptian stamp, which had sixteen sides, and a stamp from the Gabonese Republic, which was triangular. She hoped that one day they would be worth a lot of money! Anyhow, Voula was only dreaming! She was not very passionate about stamp collecting, and her interest lasted only a couple of years. Confucius, the Chinese philosopher, says it does not matter how slowly you go, so long as you don't stop. But, Voula lost interest in her stamp collecting and stopped! Thank God she didn't become *obsessive* about stamps! (1124 words)

a spoon collection

two of Voula's favourite stamps

Chapter 16
The Woodshed

In the back yard, there was a laundry, garage, outside toilet (also known as *the outhouse*) and a woodshed. They were all joined together. The woodshed had wood in there that was used to burn for the fireplace and the stove. It was about two and a half metres wide and long and maybe two metres high. Its walls were made of old fence palings with gaps between them, and it had a flat iron roof. Peter, who was adventurous, soon learnt to climb on the shed roof. As he got older he could jump off it onto a long, soft pile of grass below. From the shed roof he could also climb onto the higher roof of the garage. Whenever a ball got on the roof, Peter would climb up and get it. He was not afraid of heights!

To cut wood for the kitchen stove, chunks of wood were placed on a stump in an upright position and then chopped with an axe into smaller pieces that could fit into the stove's burner. With their dad watching, Peter and Voula were allowed to chop wood as they got older and stronger.

One day the kids were playing *Hidey*. One of the boys had the "good" idea to move some wood, and make a gap to climb inside the woodshed: it may have been Peter or maybe it was his best friend, Bob. Anyway, for *Hidey*, Peter, Bob and Jimmy hid inside the woodshed! They had

the woodshed and the pile of stacked wood inside

The fence between the neighbour and the back of the garage is falling apart: only the neighbour's corrugated iron fence holds the timber palings in place.

The woodshed is in the background on the left. There is the grassy pile Peter would jump onto. Voula is holding Sophia, her doll from Greece.

made a little room inside. Voula looked for a long time and couldn't find them. It was a really clever hiding place! This game was repeated over the next few weeks and then, while passing the woodshed, Voula heard some voices: the boys were in the woodshed! When she tried to get in, she found her way blocked by a wall of piled timber. The boys had moved the wood against the walls of the shed and left an empty place in the middle to make a little room! They could relax in there! Inside they had moved a few pieces of wood to be chairs and a table. They even had three glasses of soft drink and some of their footy cards to look at. Now they were in the middle of a game of Monopoly! Voula was amazed as well as impressed.

When the boys heard Voula trying to get into their hiding place, they moved some of the wood to the front of the shed to block her way. Then they moved the wood away from the back fence of the shed and got out. They walked along between the neighbour's fence and the back of the shed and garage to get away from Voula. They got away, but she had finally found their hiding place!

When Argyro heard about her children building a *room* in the woodshed, she was worried! She told them that it was too dangerous and that the wood could fall on them and hurt or kill them. She said they were not allowed to enter the shed again. So for a long time the kids kept away from the shed, although Voula often walked past and looked at it very thoughtfully. She was planning to disobey her Mum and go in there!

A little time later, the *Hidey* game was on again, and the only hiding places Voula could think of were some of the garden bushes. Voula ran out of ideas. The boys had sticks that they used to poke into the bushes and one exciting time Peter just missed pushing his stick onto Voula's back, but he didn't see her! Voula had looked right into Pete's eyes and felt sure he had seen her! But no! Amazingly, he kept moving along poking here and there, and she was glad she had stayed calm and had not run out of her hiding place to escape the boys. They were getting tired of searching for her. She didn't answer when they called her! The boys soon moved away to the front of the woodshed, calling out that if she was in there, they would tell their mother and she would be in trouble. They even climbed in and had a look, but Voula was not there. When her brothers went around to the front of the house to look for her there, she quickly ran out of her hiding spot in the bush, and carefully climbed over the wood into the woodshed! Naughty girl! She made it safer by quietly moving the wood around, and then she stayed there for ages.

When the boys got bored and gave up looking for her, she went into the house to find them. "Where have *you* been?" they asked her, but she refused to tell them. The woodshed was not allowed, so of course she didn't want to shed any light on *that*! She now had a great secret hiding place that she enjoyed keeping to herself. Voula wouldn't tell about the woodshed, no matter how often her brothers asked her! Whenever she was upset and felt like crying, she hid in there until she felt better. At other times Voula just enjoyed the smell of the wood and the earth, and having her own private place to herself. She really enjoyed going in there when it rained, as she could hear the noisy rain falling on the iron roof: it was very loud, but somehow, comforting. Mothers can't watch their children twenty-four seven, and it was lucky that Voula didn't get hurt in the woodshed, when a wall of wood fell around her. She jumped out of the way, only squashing her shoe.

Another game the kids played was *Find the Treasure*. Some other boys in the neighbourhood had showed it to them. Peter and Bob were keen to play it again, so they explained it to Jimmy, Voula and to Peggy and her brothers. That means there were seven kids playing. The game was very exciting and took a lot of time to play. There had to be two teams, a prize and a time limit. The seeking team had to stay at home for 15 minutes and not look outside: they had to be honest, which didn't always work very well. Honesty was not always the best policy! Then the other team used a piece of chalk to draw arrows, in difficult to find places. When the seeking team found the arrows they would follow them to find the "treasure", which was usually a block of chocolate! The game took the kids about one kilometre or so around the block of houses, and could last a couple of hours. It was very exciting and Prince, the family dog, usually came along too. Sometimes he found the other team! If the seeking team was good at finding the arrows and see the other team, they all had to run back home because the first team back were the winners. But it was a bit difficult for the *whole of one team* to return home before the other team, as the littler children couldn't run very fast. If however, the seeking team could *not* find the treasure, then the other team ate it themselves. That happened a lot! (12171 words)

the chocloate treasure

Hard-to-find, but large chalk arrows guided the way to the "chocolate treasure". The kids had to be honest when drawing the arrows, and not draw them in places too hard to find!

Hiding was a favourite children's game.

Chapter 17
The Hamilton Show

Hamilton is proud of all the things their farmers grow and especially the high quality of the sheep. Hamilton believes it is the "Current Wool Capital of the World". The Merino sheep found in Hamilton had come from Spain long ago. Unlike many of the other European animals brought to Australia, these Merino sheep loved it here and they could cope with the Australian heat. In past years, the Australian economy was "built on the sheep's back", because many countries wanted to buy Merino wool.

Merinos have the best wool. It is thick fleece and fine too, so it is great for making high quality clothes. Farmers in the Western District of Victoria, of which Hamilton is the capital city, are very proud of their sheep. They decided to make a club called the *Hamilton Pastoral and Agricultural Society*. The Society runs the *Hamilton Show* every year. It is a time when farmers can show their farm animals and share farming ideas with each other. Shows in city centres are popular in Australia, and are also for entertainment and business information. Nowadays, the *Hamilton Show* has changed its name to *Sheepvention*: a blended word, combining "sheep" and "convention". Sheepvention is a two-day event. It is held at the Hamilton Showgrounds on Shakespeare Street every year. Farmers can sell their

The Hamilton Show, 1911
Creator: George Walker   Museum Victoria   http://collections.museumvictoria.com.au/items/766724

Hamilton still prides itself on being the current wool capital of the world.

a Merino sheep

sheep and get some money. There are competitions and fashions, as well as fun rides and music.

Back in the 1960s, Jimmy, Peter and Voula were always very excited to go to the *Hamilton Show*, because there were many interesting things to see there. It felt like a carnival, just like you get in the big cities during the *Royal Melbourne Show* or the *Sydney Royal Easter Show*. Both of these big Shows were started by farmers too. They are still about sheep,cows, fashion, games and jam-making and cake competitions. Also, there are sheep dog competitions, to find the dog that can most quickly and gently put sheep together in a group and make them go into a pen. Another popular competition is wood chopping, to find the man who is the fastest to cut his log with an axe. There are the usual stalls like the carnival clown heads, windmills and Kewpie dolls on sticks. Don't forget the free showbags! It's not often you get something for nothing.

Some stalls had games to play and you could win a prize. The kids paid to get 3 balls each and then put the balls in a clown's mouth. But they could never get the balls to go into the big numbers to win a large stuffed toy. They tried to let go of each ball at the right time, but it was always wrong and the balls sometimes got stuck and slowed down. It was always just bad luck! The windmills were better value for money because they lasted longer than the games. The kids would spin around fast to make "wind". After a while it would get loose and fall off its stick. However, the best value of all were the Kewpie dolls because Argyro liked them and kept them in her bedroom, on her mirror as decorations. They had colourful, glittery dresses. Voula was not allowed to play with them, but she could still look at them in her mother's bedroom.

One year the family bought tickets to go inside a tent with the sign "Samson the Strongman". Inside were long wooden seats and the ground was covered with sawdust. Inside they saw Samson, dressed in an old-fashioned

wood chopping

a pinwheel windmill

a carnival clown head

a sledge hammer

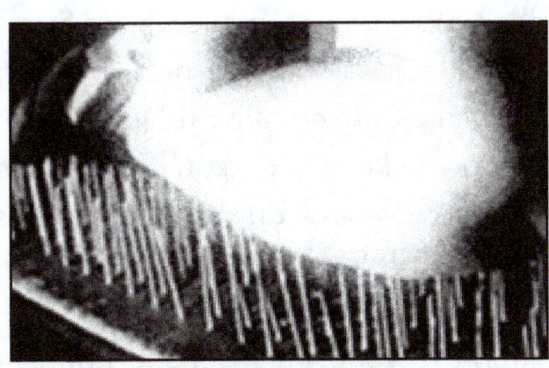

laying on a bed of nails

bathing costume, and when he was introduced, everyone clapped. He started his show by holding up some *razor blades* and warning the people watching NEVER to try to copy him. Samson then put the blades into his mouth and started chewing them! Voula felt sick! His tongue must be bleeding. "Please spit them out!" she whispered. But no, Samson kept on chewing the blades. Finally he swallowed the razor blades! Well that's what it looked like, but maybe it was a trick. We all know that what the eyes see, the heart believes!

Next, a platform of sharp nails was brought in from the back of the tent and Samson walked over and lay on top of it. He looked like a man lying on his bed. Another man came with a *sledgehammer*. A piece of timber was put on top of Samson and then a large rock on top of the timber.

The man with the sledgehammer started hitting the rock. Samson held his breath and tightened his tummy, but made no sound. Everyone was worried about him. The banging of the sledgehammer made a lot of noise on the rock until it broke. When the pieces of rock and the timber were removed from Samson, he stood up and shook hands with the man holding the sledgehammer. Samson thanked him and told him that he was okay. Next thing you know, Samson lay back on the bed of nails, the timber was back on top of him and someone drove a car on him. It was all too much for Voula!! She just wanted to get out of there. Luckily it was the end of the show and then everyone went out soon afterwards. But Argyro was proud to learn that Samson was a Greek! She wanted to take her children over to meet him. The kids never forgot Samson, the Strong Man. (If you want some more information about Samson scan this QR code

A free thing to see at the Hamilton Show was the Scottish dancing. The kids liked to stand next to a wooden dance floor that was held up on four big wooden kegs. As a bagpiper, dressed in a Scottish kilt, started up his bagpipes, pretty girls also dressed in kilts, stepped up onto the wooden platform. The girls looked very special in their *tartan kilts*. On their kilt skirts they wore lovely pins. The tartan patterns of their kilts showed their family name, because each family had a different pattern. When the bagpipe music started, the girls would begin to dance. Often they put two swords on the floor so they criss-crossed one another. Then the girls danced over the swords, and they did not trip or touch them once! While they danced and jumped in the air, the wooden floor creaked and bounced up and down. They wore pumps

left: the Wallace clan tartan right: the MacLeod tartan

left: some kilt pins

4 wooden kegs like this one held up a wooden dance floor

on their feet like ballerinas and they had a lot of skill and energy, pointing their toes and holding their hands and fingers up in the air. Sometimes the girls danced alone and at other times in pairs or more. The best dancers won first prize, usually a blue ribbon. It was all very beautiful and of course Voula dreamed that maybe she could take some ballet lessons and grow up to be a ballerina some day! (1136 words)

A Scottish girl in her kilt is dancing over swords and holding her hand up with her thumb and second finger together.

a Scotsman playing the bagpipes

Chapter 18
Going for Sunday Drives

It was Sunday and a beautiful, sunny day with a clear blue sky. It is an Aussie tradition to go for a Sunday drive, so Andy Hadis and Theo decided to visit their Greek friends who also ran a café. Their friends lived in Portland, by the sea, on the southern coastline of Victoria. They wanted to discuss work and perhaps ask them if their business was going okay. At this time cafes were losing customers, because hotels had started cooking "counter-lunches." Lucas Café was not making much money, as it had lost business to the pubs that had begun to serve lunches. It seemed like their business was going nowhere. Maybe they could all talk about it and come up with a good idea together, as without advice plans fail, but with many advisers they succeed.

Andy had a 1956 Holden he had named Spiro. Theo and *his* family and Andy and *his* family all crowded into his car! It would take a drive of about an hour and a half, down the Henty Highway. It was named after the man who first settled in the Portland area with his family, Edward Henty, in 1834. He dug the land and grew the first wheat crop too. The first person to start living in the Melbourne area was John Batman in 1835, so you see Portland was the first European settlement in Victoria!

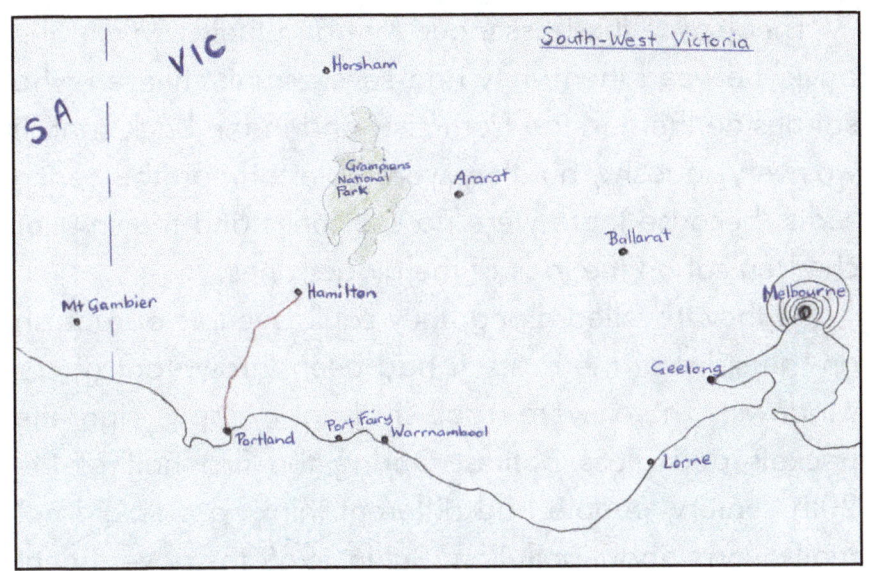

the road from Hamilton to Portland in red

the front car bench seat of a 1965 Ford Falcon (with a pom-pom hanging off the mirror)

Theo sat in the passenger seat and their wives in the back. Between them they had seven small children who sat beside them in the front seat and in the back seat. It was very squashy, but they were able to fit on the bench seats, because there were no seat belts and the smaller children sat on the laps of the bigger ones.

As they travelled along, they could see lots of rubbish on the sides of the road. It had been thrown out of car windows. There were rubbish bags, empty cigarette packets and glass bottles. During the first half of the 20th century, people had different thinking and did not really worry about pollution. But in 1969 the government started televisions commercials and advertisements like: "Keep Australia Beautiful," and, "Do the right thing" and "Tidy Towns."

Portland is about 85km from Hamilton, so when they arrived there the children felt stiff. They wanted to run free, so out they went to play along the beach. The kids were having fun running on the sand and grassy area. They took off their shoes and socks and felt the cool sand between their toes. It felt good. They laughed and they played with the waves on the beach. Voula didn't see the bee in the grass until she stepped on it and it stung her. She cried with pain. Argyro took the bee stinger out but her daughter's foot was sore, red and swollen. They went to their friend's café for ice! Voula could not run for the rest of the day and was miserable, sitting still with the adults all day long.

Another time Theo and Andy drove to Portland, Theo took his daughter along as well, for an outing. She sat in the back seat behind her father. It was all going very nicely with a few songs sung along the way. Then Theo decided to have a cigarette. He lit up and threw the dead match out of the window. To save Andy the work of emptying out the car's ash tray, Theo flicked his cigarette ash out of his window. Voula had opened her window to get some fresh air in the car, because she hated breathing in the smoke from her dad's cigarettes. Unluckily, Theo's cigarette ash flew back into the car ,through Voula's window, and onto her clothes. Voula looked down and saw some sparks of fire were burning holes in her collar. When she cried out

the grassy beach at Portland and the main road

fossicking along the cliffs

a ford sedan with Venetians on the rear window

for help Andy stopped the car on the side of the road and Theo jumped out to check what was happening. He put out the fires with his hands and double checked that they were truly out. He looked a bit shocked and didn't smoke in the car after that.

Port Fairy and Warrnambool were also favourite locations for the families, but again it was always hot and cramped in Andy's car with everyone sitting on top of each other. At Warrnambool, the Twelve Apostles were a wonderful sight (even though there were only nine of them)! The rocks and pools were fun to jump onto. Along the cliffs were many little bones of sea creatures, which had died long ago. Digging for these bones with a little pick or with a strong stone was another popular thing to do to pass the time.

About 16km west of Hamilton are the Wannon Falls and to the north of Hamilton, about 77km and an hour and twenty minutes away, are the Grampians, with hundreds of steps leading down to waterfalls and rocks. It was unusual if someone did not fall or get injured, as the children ran excitedly from one place to another. They were thrilled by the loud noise of the waterfalls and enjoyed the cool water on their toes, after running around on the rocks in the sunshine. There was always so much to see and do! (887 words)

Argyro holding Jimmy, at Wannon Falls

Mrs. Hadis and Argyro with their children at Wannon Falls

Chapter 19
Guy Fawkes Night

All the neighbours were getting their garden rubbish. They were making a big heap outside Theo's house, on the road. It was *Guy Fawkes' Night*, November 5th, and everyone was bringing wood and dry branches to put on the heap of rubbish in the middle of the road. They were building a big bonfire! The children were very excited and all afternoon they ran around finding garden rubbish and helping a lot. One of the men took control and made sure no one put anything on the heap that would smell when it burnt–like old rubber tyres.

Someone made a full-size doll of Guy Fawkes, out of paper and old clothes and put it on the heap of rubbish. There was even an old hat on its head! Guy Fawkes was the man who tried to blow up the Houses of Parliament in England, back in 1605. He was sentenced to death for his crime. So why were country people in Australia, in 1968, happy about the death of Guy Fawkes? Well it was something that many people celebrated back in the 1960s, because there were many people in Australia from Britain. Most of the children didn't understand about Guy Fawkes until they were older, but they enjoyed the excitement and the feeling of togetherness between all the neighbours.

By the time evening came around, everyone was ready

The bonfire was positioned in the middle of the road on the left side of the photo.

Every Guy Fawkes night the residents organised a bonfire.

a girl holding a sparkler

a policeman arrests Guy Fawkes

a fairy

to watch the bonfire. It was also "Cracker Night." People had bought fireworks from the Milk Bar down the road, because it was legal back then for shops to sell them. All the boys wanted to throw crackers into the bonfire: the bigger, the better! The big "Penny Bungers" were the loudest and therefore the most popular! However, Peggy and Voula liked the "sparklers" the best. Voula liked to hold a sparkler and wave it around. She pretended she was a fairy princess: some girls are like that!

As you may imagine, Peter, Voula's younger brother, had a different plan for some of his Penny Bungers. His best friend was Bob Tydon who lived across the road, and together they liked to put a tin can over a cracker, light the fuse and run away. After a few moments it made a big "boom" and the tin can went flying into the sky. A bit dangerous you might say, but lots of kids did things like that in their back yards in those days. Everyone had big blocks of land of at least a quarter of an acre. The can usually didn't go over the fence. If it did Peter and Bob would climb over the fence, like wild goats, and quickly get back their special can, ready for more fire crackers!

Voula was often left to herself, because the boys didn't want to play with a girl. Anyway she found ways to amuse herself. She had found out there were seventeen ant nests in her back yard! She got it in her mind that she should take care of them. After all, they were in *her* yard and someone had to look after them. She used to get a slice of bread and go around making tiny crumbs for the ants to find. In order to save them time and trouble, she visited each nest every day and there she would leave her gift of

A fence is easy to climb over and a hose can be a weapon.

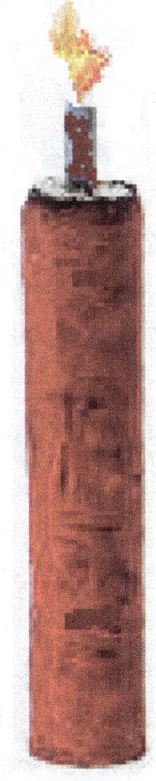

a Penny Bunger

breadcrumbs.

Voula was sure the ants appreciated it, because she sat still for hours watching them. When the crumb was first found, the ant that found it got very excited. Often it tried to move the crumb by itself, but if it couldn't it would go and get help. Ants really know how to work together! In no time at all there was a black line of ants, crawling quickly up and down to their new food. Sometimes the ants had a war with other insects and then they often carried their white baby eggs out of the nest to safety. Voula spent many hours following them to their new nests. Sometimes she helped them in their wars, by trying to find and kill their enemies. Unfortunately, she didn't see the ants' biggest enemy. It was Peter!

One day Peter decided it would be fun to *blow up* the ant nests with some crackers he had. They were left over from Cracker Night. He thought ants were not interesting and not needed in the garden. Also, it was always great to see and to hear the "bang" of a cracker. He used up all his crackers blowing up their nests and then, when he ran out of them, he used the water hose and *flooded* their nests. Bob was his helper and they were having a wonderful time together.

When his sister saw what he was doing she was very upset with him and they had a big fight, but it was too late. Most of the poor ants were dead! Voula blamed herself! She thought they had been killed just because she had made them her pets. If she had left them alone Peter would not have noticed them and planned to kill them! Fortunately, he had not found all the ant nests and

Voula was careful to feed them secretly, so Peter would not see them. She didn't like him for several days and then she forgave Peter. There is no point crying over spilt milk, is there? (895 words)

a common ant nest

Chapter 20
Pets

Most children love animals and so did Argyro's children. Since the boys didn't often play with Voula, *animals* were her playmates and friends. Many happy hours were spent watching, training and learning about these interesting creatures. Like many other families who lived in the country at that time, they had several pets. There was Mother Cat, who was always having lots of kittens, because she had never been spayed. She had a beautiful kitten named Ginger for his orange fur.

One particular day Voula was watching "Lassie" on TV. Lassie was a very clever, friendly family dog that saved her human family whenever they got into trouble. Also, Lassie obeyed commands like "sit," "come," "stay," and many other things. Argyro's family didn't have a dog yet, and Voula longed for a dog she could walk around the block, like other people. However, she only had cats, so Voula decided to teach Ginger by tying a rope round his neck and giving him instructions. Ginger was stubborn! He refused to do anything Voula tried to teach him! Next she decided to walk him around the block.

Voula carefully explained everything to Ginger and ordered him to come with her. The cat tried to pull away as it didn't like having a rope round its neck. Amazingly

Ginger hated a rope around his neck!

Lassie and her family

for Voula, her little cat friend didn't want to go for a walk with her! However, she decided he would get used to it if she showed him it was fun. Voula wanted Ginger to obey *her*, and not she to obey *him*. She ended up *dragging* poor Ginger all the way around the block! Ginger did not obey her at all, pulling against the rope all the way. When they got back home and she took the rope off Ginger, he ran away as fast as he could go! Voula felt so sorry for Ginger she never tried walking him ever again. She felt guilty. She understood that dragging a cat around by its neck was one of the worst things you could do to a cat (besides giving it a bath)! After all her effort Voula learnt one thing: cats are not like dogs, so it was not a good idea to treat Ginger like a dog.

Of course Voula also had her "pet" ants to feed and care for. Besides these cares, the family got two budgerigars, but they escaped one day by lifting up the door of their cage. First one flew out while the other lifted the cage door, then the other flew out when the door got stuck open. They were very clever really, but it had been very sad to lose them. In fact it was terrible to think that the budgies didn't love them and had wanted to get out and leave them! Argyro never got other budgies.

Instead the children got some tadpoles, which they tried to grow into frogs. They had found them in a little stream not far from home, at a place where the water was very still and didn't move much. The water was still because some sticks had got stuck together, and had made a little dam. At school Voula had been fascinated when her grade 5 teacher, Miss Slater, had shown a film

budgerigars on their perches in a cage

a film projector showing film on reels

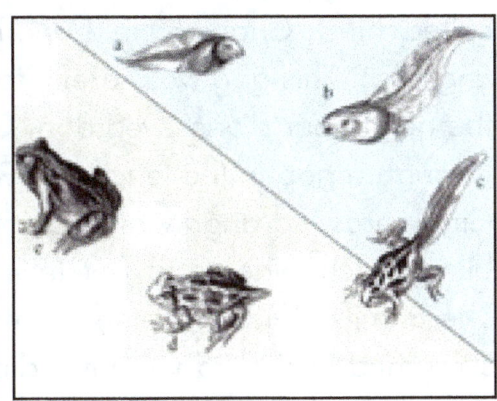
the frog life cycle

(on reels) about how tadpoles grew back legs, then front legs and then their tails fell off. It was like magic....they became frogs!

V-E-R-Y interesting indeed! So Argyro helped her children make some nets from her old stockings. Following their mother's instructions, they had tied them to long sticks and had gone looking for tadpoles. They caught some, put them in bottles with some of the water and taken them home to watch. However, there was a problem. What do you feed tadpoles? It was difficult to solve as there was no *Google* back then!

Voula and Peter tried feeding them some bread crumbs because they knew the ducks on the pond, at the Botanical Gardens, loved bread. Just to be sure they threw in some grass and bird seed too, but the tadpoles didn't become frogs at all. In fact they died. Another pet sadness for the kids!

Then, one wonderful day, the family got a medium sized, black, mongrel dog they named Prince (Theo called him "Charlie", in honour of *Prince* Charles of England). This dog was careful to look after his land and the neighbour's one-eyed dog, Cindy, a strong dog, got through a gap in the fence into Prince's yard. Prince and Cindy growled angrily at each other and then attacked, biting each other and not letting go of their mouths. The Shmitz children, Peter, Jimmy and Voula called and screamed at their dogs but it didn't help. It seemed the dogs wanted to kill each other! Argyro finally heard the noise and came out, as did Mrs. Shmitz. Argyro turned the water on the hose and started wetting the dogs,

a pigeon coop

2 pigeon eggs *a couple of fledglings*

a mating pair

which startled them enough so that everyone was able to separate them. The hole in the fence was carefully fixed and Prince and Cindy had to be happy just growling and barking at each other.

Next came Peter's pigeons. Now, Bob across the road had a lot of pigeons and as Peter was his best mate, Pete learnt a lot about caring for them and racing them against other pigeon owners. There was a pigeon club that met monthly to release their pigeons and race them, to see whose pigeons arrived home first or second etc. Peter told Jimmy and Voula there were pigeons that could catch and invite other pigeons back to their home with them. There were also racing pigeons that were fast flyers. However, all the birds would return home: they were "homing pigeons". When Peter released them, they would fly around their home once or twice to remember how to get back. After that they would take off, flying around in the sky for an hour or so, before returning home. If they were late the boys worried, because they thought maybe someone's pigeon would try to lead their birds to its own home.

Bob gave Peter his first two pigeons to start him off, and Argyro helped Peter make a cage for them by changing the outdoor loo. They used chicken wire to make the cage. In it they built shelves and made boxes for the pigeons to build their nest in. Also, to make the birds happy, they added some perches, as well as a landing platform in front of the opening into the cage.

Before long the pigeons mated, two eggs were laid and the parents were trying to hatch them. Peter went

a fledgling pigeon

into the cage to inspect the eggs. Soon after that the pigeons pushed their eggs out of the nest. They smashed on the concrete floor below. Bob told Peter that he shouldn't touch the eggs, as the parents smell humans and destroy their eggs out of fear. It was very sad because the little birds had already started growing inside their shell houses. Next time they made their pair of eggs no one was allowed near them, until the happy day Peter ran into the kitchen to tell his mum that he had babies!

metal leg rings

Everyone went to the cage to see the baby pigeons. Yep, two living, chirping, featherless, and pretty ugly-looking little pigeons sat in a nest. The family stayed well back to avoid any problems. However, sometimes a baby was pecked to death by its own sibling or parent. Maybe only one was enough for the parents. It seemed very harsh to Voula, but nature is tough. The strong baby birds soon grew fluffy feathers, but different ones from the adult feathers of their parents.

Peter started breeding the pigeons and ended up

with about twenty-five Homing Pigeons. He bought little numbered metal rings, from the pigeon club, and put them on their legs to identify them, and Peter as their owner. In no time, Bob and Peter had a little business going on, as more eggs were hatched and baby pigeons grew up. Peter's friends bought some of his pigeons because breeding pigeons looked like a lot of fun.

One day Peter and Voula were told to clean the cage floor of all the bird poo. They had to shovel the thick, stinky poo off the cage floor, into a wheel barrow. Then wheel it to an unused part of the back yard and throw it out. It was good for the garden plants after it dried out a bit! When the bird poo was gone, they used the water hose to wash the floor. The pigeons did poo a lot and when the cage floor was completely covered, the kids had to get rid of it again.

To make sure the birds were out of the way while they cleaned the cage, the pigeons were let out of their cage to fly around. The young pigeons were taken out of their nests and cared for by Voula, as she sat on the grass in the front yard, well away from the cage in the back. She had five young pigeons in her lap. She looked at them. They were old enough to touch without the parents killing them. For some reason as the birds got a bit older the parents didn't mind if humans picked up their young. The children had found out this fact when they picked up a baby off the floor where it had fallen. They put it back in its nest. They had waited to see if its parents would kill it, but they had accepted it and fed it. So, now Voula held the babies without fear of hurting them as she lovingly stroked them. She touched their ears and twisted their necks around to see how far they could turn; it was about 270 degrees!

Voula started thinking how she could help Peter with his pigeons. Out of the blue, she hit on a good idea: she could *train* them to be the best, strongest flyers by training them early! Then Peter's pigeons would become famous for being the best and fastest racing pigeons in Hamilton! They would be like "super pigeons" and Peter would win his races against Bob's experienced pigeons. Peter would be happy about that and she would be in his good books.

While Peter was busily hosing out and cleaning the pigeon cage, Voula carefully took the baby pigeons off her skirt and onto the grass. She knelt beside them and spoke soft, loving words to take away their fears. Then, one by one, she picked them up into her cupped hands and gently threw them up a few centimetres—so far so good. They would flap their skinny wings trying to keep their balance. Voula knew that using their little wings would help their muscles to grow. In her mind she could see them growing up to be super pigeons! Stronger than their parents were and smarter too!

She patiently exercised each of the five birds and then she started at the beginning again and repeated their exercises. It was important not to get bored. When she stopped to rest, she found that the birds were looking tired and droopy. She would continue their exercises tomorrow. "Too much exercise," thought Voula. "Next time I should go slower." As she looked at them, she got very worried because the little birds drooped even more.

Finally, one after the other, they stopped breathing! She was in shock! She was scared that Peter would be very sad and angry with her. Perhaps he would hit her! What would he say?

Maybe she wouldn't tell him about her exercise classes for the birds and he wouldn't be upset with her. However, Voula felt so guilty, she had to tell the truth to him. She went to find him in the back yard where he had nearly finished cleaning the pigeon cage. She told him she had been trying to help him, to have the best pigeons ever. Then she took him to the grass where she had left the dead birds. When Peter looked at their bodies, he was very sad and Voula explained she had tried to strengthen them, but it had all gone wrong! Peter was certainly not happy, but he did not hit her, and he did something worse: he told her to keep away from his pigeons. He said she was not allowed to come near them again!! Anyhow, that lasted a few days and then he forgave her. After all, he liked the help Voula could give him with shovelling the bird poo and keeping the cage clean.

The next time she got involved with the pigeons was when she heard Peter calling for help. That day Voula was with Mother Cat and her newest kittens, in the outside laundry, near the pigeon cage. Peter came running in with a white face, "My pigeon is stuck in some wire and she's bleeding. I can't get her down. Do something Voula!" They went to check the situation together. About a metre above their heads was Peter's special pigeon "catcher" that could invite other pigeons into the cage. They saw that some cage wire had gone through the bird's foot, just above its claw. It couldn't move anywhere. It was held down by the wire in its leg, even though it had tried to get away from Voula as she got near the injured bird. Peter got a pair of pliers but couldn't cut the wire because he didn't want to see his bird suffer. He told Voula, "Come on Voula. You can do it, you're tough!" She knew this was her big chance to help her capable, younger brother. Voula felt she should not fear failure, but rather fear not trying! She took the pliers from him, climbed up the cage a bit, gritted her teeth and cut the wire.

Peter took the bird. "Do you think it's going to live?" he asked uncertainly: this was his favourite pigeon. Voula tried to sound confident, "Yeah, she'll be alright." Together with Peter they held the bird and prepared a bath of water mixed with pink Condy's crystals to disinfect the leg.

Over the next few days, the kids watched the bird as it flew about in the cage. The other birds didn't want it near them. It was a great relief when the foot healed, but it stayed swollen and the bird hopped when it walked on the ground. Peter was very grateful to Voula for her help and even said he could not have saved the bird without her. He told Voula she had saved the pigeon's life. That was music to Voula's ears, as Peter did not often give her praise. It didn't matter that the bird's leg was unusable because it was alive. Voula had Peter's respect. "This is the beginning of a great friendship with my brother!" thought Voula. Do you think she was right? (2500 words)

Jimmy with Peter's adolescent pigeons and below with an adult one.

the pidgeon with the damaged leg

When Peter and Voula were 8 and 9, people thought they were twins.

Chapter 21
The Billy-Cart

It was Saturday morning and Voula was looking for something to do. From inside the house, she could hear the banging sounds of a hammer. She followed the noise out into the back yard. The banging was coming from inside the old garage. The wooden door of the garage had fallen off, and had been left leaning on the side wall of the garage, until Theo had enough time to fix it, so it was easy for her to look inside. What did she see? Peter and his friend Bob Tydon, who lived across the road, were busily nailing together bits of wood: long pieces of timber and shorter ones too. They also had four wheels, about 20 cm in diameter, waiting on the old table they were working on. It looked very interesting. She hoped that maybe they would let her be part of their plans!

"Whatsha doin' boys?" asked Voula. "Makin' a billy-cart!" was Bob's short reply. "Ooh, can I help too?" asked Voula hopefully. "Nah! This is boy stuff!" Voula left them to their business. They were banging and nailing all afternoon.

When they finally came out from the garage, they were pulling a strong-looking billy-cart behind them. It looked plain and simple, but it's the foundation that stands the test of time! Now they wanted to find out how good their foundation really was! "Who's going down the Hill first?"

asked Peter hoping to be the one. "I will," answered Bob, "but only if you want me to." "OK!" agreed Peter. Peter had great respect for Bob who was two years older than he was.

Their houses were in Byron Street, named after the famous English poet and lover of Greek art. Argyro had told her children about Lord Byron and they thought it was quite good to live in a street with his name. Happily for Peter and Bob, Byron Street also had a famous neighbourhood hill, Billy Goat Hill, just outside their front gates. Some people think the hill was named because of some goats kept on an empty block behind Bob's house. Billy Goat Hill in Byron Street is only a hill, not a big mountain, but to the kids in the neighbourhood it was big enough! The billy-cart would go down very, very fast.

Peter and his mate, Bob, parked the billy-cart on top of the hill. They knew the road rules, so they kept it on the left side of the road. Unfortunately, the boys had a small problem: their billy-cart didn't have any brakes! How would they stop the billy-cart? Well they would use their feet! By dragging them along the road, they hoped to slow down and slowly stop their billy-cart. Peter, whose idea it was to make the billy-cart, gave Bob this advice: "Bob, just stop by putting your feet down on the road." Bob looked a bit scared but he was a brave boy. He wanted to prove Peter could trust him to drive their billy-cart, and to prove that their billy-cart was a good one. Nothing would stop Bob from going down that hill!

Well, I reckon about twelve kids got together to watch Bob go down Billy Goat Hill for its first drive! It was very exciting for everyone. The kids there were: Bob's big sister, the three Shmitz kids from next-door, a couple of boys from down the road, Peter, Voula, Jimmy and the four Hadis children. Maybe there were one or two others but it's hard to say. It was a day to remember! All the kids knew it was a big step, being in a "vehicle" on the road like an adult!

Where were the parents you might ask? In those days kids were often left to themselves. Most of the time parents had no idea what their kids were up to. As long as they were around the neighbourhood, it was okay. "Quality time" for parents and kids had not been created yet: parents worked while children played together.

Some of the kids were jealous and told Bob that the billy-cart wouldn't work properly. However, they waited to see in case the billy-cart *would* work well. If it did, then some of them wanted to drive the billy-cart too! You must understand that Hamilton is a country town. There is not very much traffic in residential streets; especially on weekends when all the shops closed at noon on Saturday. In those days no one worked, or played sport, on Sundays. Therefore, it was a *fair bet* that no cars would be on the road when Bob rode down Billy Goat Hill.

Bob held the rope tightly in his hands. Next he tested the cart. When he pulled the rope with his left hand, the front wheels indeed turned left. When he tugged it with his right hand, the wheels turned to the right. After that he checked the brakes: he was wearing his strong leather boots. He was ready! Peter started the countdown as Bob sat seriously on the billy-cart, staring straight ahead, "10,

9, 8, 7, 6..." All the other kids joined in, "...5, 4, 3, 2, 1 TAKE OFF!"

Bob pushed on the road with his boots! The cart was slow at first but quickly picked-up speed as it went down the hill. Now he was flying! Everyone knew there was no way Bob could stop, even if he wanted to, because he was going too fast!

At the bottom of the hill was the intersection of Byron

In the back yard was the outdoor laundry. On the left side is the new washing machine with its hand rotated wringers [beside a copper water-boiler heated by log fire].

On the right is the garage with its broken door leaning on the wall and inside can be seen the old table where the boys built their billy-cart.

There were some Billy Goats on an empty block at the top of Billy Goat Hill.

Photographer: Armin Kubelbeck, CC-BY-SA, Wikimedia Commons

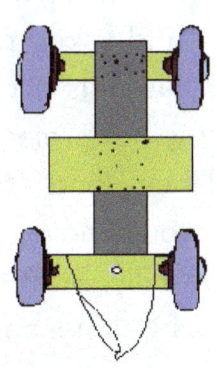

Peter's billy-cart was nailed together.

Street and Goldsmith Street. *As luck would have it*, just as Bob got closer to the intersection, Voula could see another vehicle on Goldsmith Street, coming towards Billy Goat Hill. Oh, no! Poor Bob might be killed! Bob saw the car and he must have felt his death was near! What could he do? The kids watching him held their breath and waited to see what would happen. Quickly pulling the rope with his left hand Bob stuck his right foot out the side of the cart for balance. As he turned sharply to the left into Goldsmith Street, the car *just* missed him and the driver yelled out something to him! Bob was still alive! All the kids cheered. Bob had done it! He was their new hero! However, from then on, they had a new way of doing things. Someone waited at the bottom of Billy Goat Hill and waved their hand when there were no cars coming. Then the billy-cart could take-off in safety.

All the boys eagerly lined up for turns on the billy-cart to go down Billy Goat Hill. However, after what Voula had just seen with Bob, with how fast Bob went down the hill and his near-death experience, she was too scared to get on the cart. Anyway she tried to *save face*. She went to the boys and asked for a turn too. But they made it easy for her. "No girls allowed!" they decided. Voula was secretly happy, but pretended to be upset, "That's not fair!" she told them, and walked away. She hoped that one day she too would have the courage of her little brother, to go down Billy Goat Hill …. but not today. In her head she thought, "The boys really are very brave." Voula didn't know what the future held for her…she *would* get on the billy-cart, but *not* to go down Billy Goat Hill! (1238 words)

Bob's brakes!

Argyro and Peter are walking up Billy Goat Hill.

looking at the two church steeples from the top of Billy Goat Hill [circa 1928-1954]

Chapter 22
The Monorail

Voula could see that the boys always had lots of fun going down Billy Goat Hill on the billy-cart. Finally one day, she got up enough courage to ask for a ride "No way! No girls allowed!" Peter and Bob said as usual. After a few weeks of much use, the billy-cart's wheels were bent and twisted. This was because the boys were rough and often crashed the billy-cart, on purpose. Anyway, the day arrived when the cart wouldn't move any more. It was busted!

Once again, hammering was heard from the garage as Peter nailed a "backrest" on the cart, because he wanted to improve it and make it more comfortable. He tried to fix the wheels but they were too twisted. Not to worry: Peter had a plan!

The week before, Peter had seen a monorail train on the telly. It was in Disneyland, in the USA, and it was used to take people around Disneyland to look at the sights. It was part of *Tomorrow Land* and Peter had been fascinated by the monorail, so he decided to make one. Guess what he was going to use?

Peter set to work. He found an old pulley in the garage. It was a rusty pulley about 4cm in diameter, but how could he use it to make a monorail billy-cart? Well he would

Peter's billy-cart was built with a back-rest before it was changed into a "monorail".

an old, rusty pulley

Disneyland's monorail inspired Peter.

find a way; after all *necessity is the mother of invention*! All day he thought and thought. Then he hit on an idea!

Peter took the wheels off the billy-cart. Next he got some rope and tied the front and back ends of the cart in a big loop. Then he joined a second rope through the pulley and the rope holding the cart. He dragged the cart along the yard to the back fence where there was a tall plum tree, about six or seven metres high. He left the cart at the bottom of the tree and picked up a long piece of rope.

Carefully climbing the tree, Peter quickly reached the top and tied one end of the rope to a strong branch. Then he climbed back down and went in search of Bob and Jimmy. He would need help: the more hands the better. (For your information, Peter grew up and became a civil engineer.)

By the time he got back with his two helpers, Voula had also turned up. "Whatsha doin' boys?" she asked hopefully. "Making a monorail," answered Peter in a matter-of-fact way. He had climbed onto the bottom branch and while the other boys were lifting the cart, Peter was pulling it up with the rope. Voula helped to lift it too because the boys let her help. Sometimes the cart slipped down and they had to start lifting it up all over again. It was a great effort, and they were at it all afternoon, but at last the cart was tied to the pulley and hung about three metres above the ground! They all looked up at the cart and thought it looked good up there!

Peter told them his monorail was nearly ready. He then got the other end of the rope and tied it carefully to a thick post on the fence shared with the neighbour. The monorail was on the pulley and ready to go from the tree to the fence! Now *someone* had to try it to see if it would work, but who could be his guinea pig? Jimmy was the smallest and the lightest, but he refused. It looked too dangerous for him: he was a smart boy!

"Voula if you want to, you can be the first to have a turn on the monorail," Peter said kindly. Voula knew it might not work and she didn't like high places: they made her legs feel like jelly! But, at the same time, she felt honoured to be asked, because it was not often that she was invited to "play with the boys". She had recently climbed to the top of that plum tree and wasn't *as* afraid of heights as she normally was. She had always been a *chicken* when it came to heights! Voula made a quick decision. "Okay then, I'll do it!" she told the three boys.

Jimmy, Bob and Peter watched as she carefully climbed up to the branch holding the *monorail*. Then she felt scared. The monorail didn't look very strong. "Just get in!" Peter advised her. "How?" she asked him. "It swings away when I try to get in." Peter instructed her, "Put one foot in and then quickly get in and sit on the seat." Voula really wanted to get this right so she reached out with her foot and held the monorail still. Then, as quick as lightning, she sort of *fell* into the seat! However, she didn't have long to enjoy the monorail because a moment later she felt herself and the cart falling!

"Aarhhh!" Voula let out a short fearful cry. The next thing she knew, she was on the ground. The monorail had *not* slid along the rope at all! It had come straight down because the rusty pulley broke! Fear filled her heart when she felt a strange, tingle along her spine, where her back had hit the backrest. Voula was afraid to move. "I think I'm paralysed," she whispered to her brothers and Bob. She had just finished reading a book, "What Katy Did", by Susan Coolidge, about an American girl who got paralysed after falling off a high swing. Now she remembered it and thought the same thing had happened to her.

"Don't be stupid!" Peter told her. She was amazed that the boys ran away, leaving her on the ground. Voula had half-expected some sympathy from them, but now she felt angry. "They don't care about me!" she told herself. Tears fell from her eyes and her back was hurting and it was still *tingling*. She decided that the best thing to do was not to move. Maybe her mother would miss her and come and help her.

After a while, the tingling stopped, but her back still hurt a lot. Voula kept very still until she got bored of waiting. She tried to move her legs and she could do it! She wasn't paralysed after all! Slowly, carefully, she got up. Voula felt very lucky. She had thought she would be hurt and unable to walk again. She had thought she would be in a wheelchair, just like Katy in the book! (1080 words)

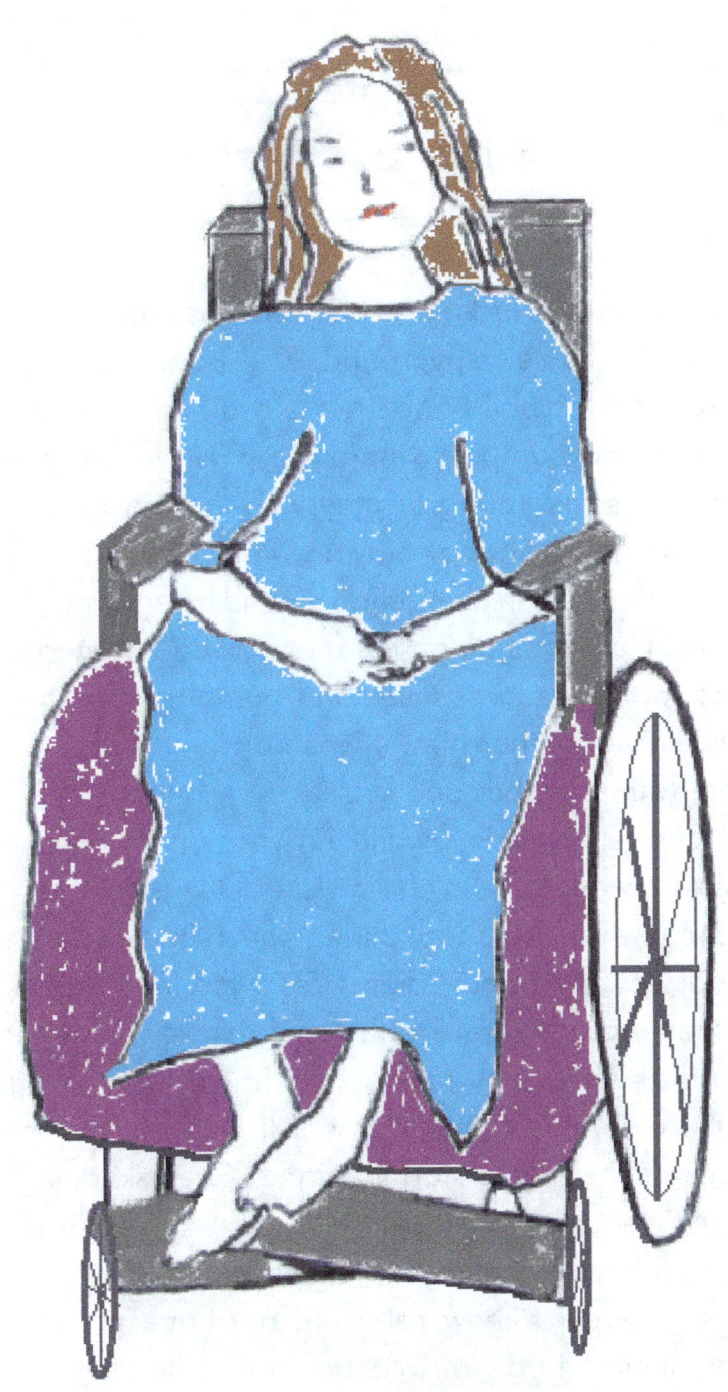

Voula thought she might end-up in a wheelchair.

Chapter 23
Sticks and Stones

Voula was lucky at school because the girls used a nice, quiet playground. The boys usually played cricket and football on the grass oval, so there was little pushing and bumping where the girls played "Skippy". Jimmy was too young to play with the big boys on the oval and he was happy playing with kids from his kinder years. Peter was an energetic boy, and he enjoyed physical games. He was often on the footy ground at school. Pete loved football and pushing and bumping with the other boys did not bother him. It was normal for him to come home with scratches and bruises.

However, one day, while Argyro was working at the café as a waitress, she had a visitor: it was Pete's teacher, who came to the shop during lunchtime. Because the school was only about 250 metres away, it was not difficult for the teacher to walk to the café. However, the teacher surprised Argyro by telling her that Peter was fighting on the oval, every day! Worse still, the teacher believed Peter was the one to start the fights! She asked Argyro to make Peter stop fighting with the other boys. Argyro was shocked because what the teacher told her was not like her son. Argyro knew Peter did not have a bad heart! Peter himself had not told her about fighting with the boys at school. Argyro decided to go to the playground and see for herself what was going on. She went during lunchtime, the very next day.

The noise of school children during playtime is familiar to all of us, but nothing prepared Argyro for what she saw. There on top of some playground equipment was Peter, with Steven Hadis and some other Greek boys beside him. They were fighting against a circle of Australian boys who were yelling rude names at them. Peter was holding a long stick and keeping away the boys attacking him. He was teasing them with the words, "Sticks and stones will break my bones, but names will never hurt me!"

Argyro could see her son was protecting himself and his friends. She felt pride that he was brave enough to stand up for himself. Peter and his friends were against a lot of kids, but they did not seem too afraid. They seemed to enjoy the challenge and to think of it as a fighting game. After all, the best method of defence is offence! If anyone could complain of bad behaviour it should be Argyro, because Peter was only trying to protect himself. Argyro went to find the Headmaster to tell him Peter was being bullied. She told him to take care of her son and stop the boys picking on him. Pete's teacher never complained again. Argyro never told Peter about her visit to the school, or her little chat with the Headmaster, until many, many years later.

Children of migrants had a few problems, because Jimmy, Voula and Peter found themselves being bullied *after* school. It happened that, as they were walking home from school one day, they were hit on their heads, chests and legs by acorns being thrown by boys hiding behind trees. It really hurt! All they could do was to use their arms to cover their faces and run away. They hoped it was just that one time, but it continued and even got worse as more boys joined in the "fun." It seemed that the playground fighting had got out onto the streets! Now it was difficult to get home from school because little groups of boys waited to throw acorns at them along the way. It became a *war game* after school, as piles of acorns were collected and used against Peter, who collected his own acorns and always fought back. Jimmy and Voula used to run away. Even Bob Tydon started helping Peter because he was Pete's friend and they often played together around the neighbourhood.

Bob and Pete didn't want to look weak, so after school, they would go down Billy Goat Hill to the oak trees in the park beside the pool. They carried bags so they could fill them with acorns to throw at the boys attacking them. When they were ready, they went looking for their "enemies" and started *shooting* their acorns at the other boys. They hid behind trees and fences when the other boys fought back. I think all the boys liked this fighting game, even though they got bruises all over their bodies.

Because neither Argyro nor Theo had a driver's licence, their children, like most children in those days, had to walk to school, about 650 meters from home. However, walking from school became a real problem, so Argyro finally told her husband, Theo, what was going on. He decided to hire a taxi, to deliver his kids to and

acorns on an oak tree

from school every weekday. This went on for about half a year and meanwhile Peter was not allowed to go out and look for acorns! After that, life returned to normal, and walking to and from school started again.

Racism was also common in the 1960s and even adults had trouble. One day when Argyro was at home and Jimmy was still a baby, she heard some stones hitting her windows and roof. The next day was the same, so she took notice of the time and waited the following day to see what would happen. Argyro saw two boys, on their way home from school, take aim at her house and throw stones they had collected for that reason. They were aged about ten years. Next day Argyro stood outside in her front yard when the boys walked proudly past. To her big surprise they threw stones at *her* and one even hit her *baby*! They quickly ran down the road, but Argyro decided to take action and followed the boys to see where they lived. She planned to talk to their parents. They had slowed down because they had not realised Argyro was following them. When they reached the park beside the Hamilton Olympic Swimming Pool, at the bottom of Billy Goat Hill, they suddenly saw her and started running.

Argyro gently put Jimmy on the grass and chased the boys. As she got closer she screamed at them never to come near her house again. They kept running and didn't look back, but she never had any trouble with them throwing stones again. In fact, one day as Argyro was walking along her street she saw a lady walking towards her. The lady was looking confused with the behaviour of her son, who was trying to hide himself behind his mother.

As the lady and Argyro passed one another, Argyro saw it was one of the boys who had thrown stones. He was now red-faced and very quiet! His mother did not know what it was all about and Argyro smiled to herself. (1159 words)

the entrance to the pool

the park next to the swimming pool

at the Hamilton Pool [summer 1962-63]

from left to right: John Hadis, Argyro's sister visiting from Melbourne, Peggy Hadis, Peter, Jimmy, Theo Hadis, Voula, Argyro's nephew Theo, and Argyro

the swimming pool plaque showing it opened in 1955

Chapter 24
The Pipe Tunnel and Prince

Voula couldn't believe her eyes! She was in the park next to Hamilton's swimming pool. She stared into the dark opening in front of her. Peter, his mate Bob and Steven Hadis had gone into the huge pipe tunnel. Out of this pipe a stream of water poured out. The pipes were about two metres wide and about the same height. Since the pipe tunnel wasn't finished, it had been left open, and the water came out of it onto the ground and continued along until it joined the Grange Burn River. It took another couple of years before the pipe tunnel was finished and covered up. However, to a child, a couple of years is a long time! Until the work was finished the children enjoyed playing there, while their parents didn't know where they were!

Now, standing in front of the tunnel, Voula watched the water as it came out of the open pipe. She remembered the boys had said they wanted to go *exploring*. Didn't they know how dangerous it was to go in the water tunnel?

After a few minutes she could hear them shouting in the pipe tunnel. They were enjoying the echo of their voices. Voula slowly walked into the tunnel and made some noises to listen to her voice too. This was fun! Maybe she could go in further. As she walked there was a sudden turn and everything became completely black. When she stretched out her hand Voula couldn't see it! This was too scary for her, so she turned around and ran outside into the daylight. However, she wanted to be brave, so she tried again. This time she picked up the family dog, Prince, for comfort and carried him into the tunnel. Still, because she couldn't see where she was walking, it really frightened her. Prince wasn't much help, because he was trying to get free: he didn't like it either. What if he could smell some danger? What if a stranger was hiding in here; or maybe a poisonous eel or a snake? She had seen eels in the stream, so she knew they could easily be in the tunnel too. No, she felt afraid and she couldn't go into the darkness; so she turned back. She couldn't hear the boys' voices any more. Where were they? Would they get out unhurt? How would she explain all of this to her mother?

After about half an hour, Steven came running towards her. To her surprise he was running *on top* of the pipes and not inside the tunnel! "How did you get out?" Voula questioned Steve. Steven explained, "There's an opening near Thompson Street outside the footy oval." Voula was still worried and asked, "Where are the others?" He told her, "They're coming back inside the tunnel but I was too scared. I got out of the opening, even though they called me a *chicken*, I didn't want to go back inside the tunnel!" Voula could understand exactly how Steven felt. He was honest; not everyone is a reckless super hero! Still it was a big surprise to hear where the boys had gone, because to get to the opening, the boys had travelled about one and a half kilometres *inside* the dark tunnel! Voula thought

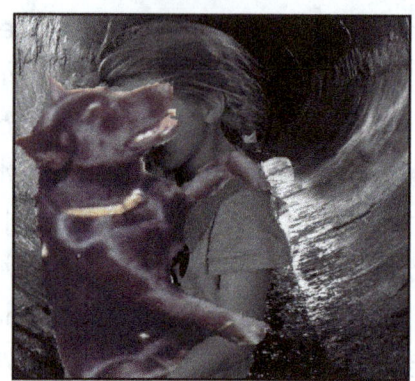

Voula goes in with Prince

an open pipe tunnel

they were crazy! It was very dangerous!

It soon became a favourite place for the boys, who often went into the pipe tunnel to play. Once the boys told Voula they saw a water snake in there and it had given them a good scare! Danger creates caution, and after that, they would ride their bikes inside the pipe tunnel: just in case another snake came along. However, when the boys rode their bikes they couldn't climb out at the other end of the tunnel, because the opening on Thompson Street had a grate, which they could climb through, but it was too small to get their bikes out. Therefore, they always had to hang a U-turn and come back to the tunnel opening, next to the swimming pool.

Sometimes Voula and Prince would go running along the stream to where it joined the Grange Burn River. A little further along, there was a bridge with no name, on Portland Road, just before it becomes the Henty Highway. Under the bridge, it was shady and peaceful. Voula enjoyed the gentle sounds of running water and the croaking of the frogs in the water grass. It was a favourite spot for Voula and Prince, but also for all the kids.

One afternoon the three Hadis brothers, Peter and Bob rode their bikes to the bridge. They saw Peggy Hadis and Voula with Prince sitting below the bridge. The girls' bikes were lying on the grass beside them as they talked and listened to the quiet sounds around them. They were pulling at the long green grass beside them. After a few minutes Peter called Prince to come to him. The dog ran up the slope and wagged his tail against Peter's leg. What did Prince look like? He was a black, mongrel dog,

the bridge with no name on Portland Road

Prince, the loved pet.

about fifty centimetres high. He was a good dog, but he didn't like water and he hated having a bath! Prince didn't know what Pete had decided to do! Peter wanted his dog to learn to swim, and there was only one way Peter knew how to do that: he picked up his pet and dropped him over the bridge into the river, three metres below!

Peggy and Voula stood up to look for Prince where he dropped into the water! They were worried about him. Bubbles came up where Prince had fallen in. He had hit the water on his belly. It must have hurt him! Poor Princey! The children all waited for him to come up out of the water, but they only saw more bubbles. Everyone felt badly for Prince, even Peter had his doubts! They started calling their dog repeatedly and hoping he could hold his breath under water for what seemed like a long time.

Just when everyone thought Prince had drowned, he suddenly popped his head out of the water. The girls called to him as he swam to the water's edge. However, he didn't come to the girls for some hugs. Prince ran up the slope and ran away from the children. He was frightened and maybe Prince thought the kids had tried to kill him!?

From that time, his personality changed. Prince was never the same again. Their dog became angry and more aggressive. Whenever a car drove by the house, Prince would jump over the one meter fence and chase after it. Then he would bite the back tyre and not let go until the wheel had turned him round and round two or three times. After that he would let go of the tyre and fall on the road, barking loudly at the departing car.

He also barked at *people* walking past the house and most times he would jump the fence and attack their shoes and ankles. Whenever this happened the children tried to stop him, but of course someone complained to the Dog Pound. The *Dog Catcher* came to their front door. He wore an Akubra hat and held a dangerous looking rifle over his shoulder. He knocked on the door loudly, and when the scared kids saw him in the doorway, they ran to get their mother.

Argyro was shocked to see a man with a rifle at her front door. When he ordered her to give him their dog, she shouted at him, "Get out! Go away!" After some arguing he left, but he warned Argyro that he would be back to *shoot* the dog, if he had any more complaints from people. Sadly, about four years later, Prince finally did die, but he wasn't killed by the Dog Catcher! Prince was chasing after another dog, when he ran across Bell Street, a busy road in Melbourne, and got hit by a car. He crawled back onto the footpath where Voula and Argyro, had chased after him. They couldn't do anything to help Prince. He died while Voula spoke his name with a trembling voice and patted him. Poor Prince! He had lived a short but exciting life! (1381 words)

Prince used to chase cars passing by the house.

a rifle and an Akubra hat

Chapter 25
The Bike

Holding onto the picket fence with her left hand, Voula sat carefully on Peter's bike trying to keep her balance. She was finding it very difficult to learn how to ride a bike, but as her parents had promised her a new bicycle, if she could learn to ride, she kept trying. So now here she was holding the neighbour's front fence. She was able to sort-of-ride by holding onto the right handle bar with her right hand, while pushing off and trying to turn the pedals a bit. Then she would suddenly hold onto the front fences of the next neighbour's house while she slowly rolled a small way along and fell leftwards onto the fences. At the moment she was holding Mrs. Manning's fence, about a hundred metres from her house, but it had taken her about half an hour to get there!

Voula wished she could already ride! Why could her younger brother, Pete, ride and not she? Let's face it, Peter had put in many hours of practice and now he could ride without even holding on to the handle bars! He was such a show-off! Also he could ride fast …down Billy Goat Hill! Voula was proud of him but she REALLY wanted to be able to ride too.

Voula continued her efforts all the way to the corner and then had to turn left to continue around the block. However, she now had two problems: the street was downhill and there were also thorny branches along a low wire fence. She had nothing to hang on to, while she tried to steer the bike and push it along at the same time. Voula had another problem because if she turned around to ride back towards home, she would have to hold the handle bar with her left hand and hold onto the fences with her right hand. She was right-handed and so her weaker left hand would have to control the bike. Oh well, she decided it was easier to go back home than to try going downhill, without any fence to help her keep her balance. Also if she crossed the road, several fences were not high enough to hold on to.

By the time Voula got back to her house, her hands

the bikes were put against the broken garage door leaning against the garage wall

and legs had been hurt banging against the fences. She was covered with scratches and bruises, but she felt that she had improved her riding skills a lot! She could stay on the bike and turn the pedals a couple of times without holding on to any fences.

A few weeks later she was riding Peter's bike quite well, but unluckily she had bent the handle of the bike bell against a fence. Peter wasn't happy that his new bike got damaged by his big sister, so it was good when Argyro and Theo bought Voula a bike for her eleventh birthday. It was pink and later had a white basket put on the front handlebars.

Voula could finally ride very well, even without holding the handles, just like her younger brother, but not fast down Billy Goat Hill. Commonly, in those days bikes didn't have gears and to stop you pushed backwards on the pedals. It was very easy to understand and use.

Voula and Peter used to keep their bikes in the back yard, leaning against the broken wooden garage door. One morning Voula and Peter had an argument about something. I don't know what! When Voula walked into the back yard she saw Peter's bike, with its bent bell, resting in its usual place. It was then she thought of a naughty plan to *get even* with him. She secretly let the air out of his back bicycle tyre! In the afternoon, Peter ran to his bike, as he planned to go for a ride to the local milk bar to get some football cards (they came inside bubble gum packets with photos of football players). Because Peter was often doing naughty things himself, he realised straight away that it was his sister who had given him a flat tyre. He looked at Voula and told her he knew *she* had let the air out of his tyre! Now she would be in trouble! Voula found it hard to lie and her face looked guilty! She told him the truth and that *he* made her do it! This made Peter VERY angry!

Soon Voula *saw* that he was getting angry because the colour of his face changed from pink to dark red to almost purple! She walked backwards away from him, but Peter was furious and punished his sister by kicking and bending the spokes of Voula's new bike. She told her mother, but Argyro didn't want to take sides in their fighting. Voula pretended she didn't care, so she didn't play with her bike for a few days. Then she went out and straightened the wheel spokes as much as she could. She washed her bike and made it shine, but it was no longer perfect. She should not have wronged Peter and now she had to live with the problems she had caused. It was a good lesson to learn: don't plan to do bad things to others, because bad things will happen to you too!

A few of the neighbourhood kids had bikes and so did one or two of the Hadis children. Therefore, they used to go riding out of Hamilton and into the local paddocks. Voula helpfully put the family dog, Prince, in her wire basket so she could give him a rest. However, his paws got sore on the wire and he wriggled, making the handle bars turn and Voula crashed. Sometimes Voula used to dink Peggy on her bike, until she too got her own bike. In this way the kids explored beautiful, shady spots and sometimes went "mushrooming", but they were never sure if the mushrooms they found were safe to eat. It was just fun to jump on toadstools and mushrooms and squash them into the ground. Why is that?

Another time, the group of kids, some on bikes and some on foot, found an old wooden bridge with a railway track going over it. While some of the friends had a rest and a bit of a picnic on the grass below the bridge, Peter, Bob Tydon and Steven Hadis decided to go across the bridge. Isn't that what it was there for? Sure, it takes courage to try new things, but it takes wisdom to accept you *can't* do everything. Anyway the boys didn't have much wisdom....they were too young. They were jumping around and happily pushing each other, as they jumped across the wooden beams of the railway line. Suddenly they stopped playing and looked very scared. They had heard a train and it was coming straight towards them! What could they do? They had seen that every now and then, there were some parts on the bridge that you could go to, if you needed to get out of the way of a coming train. The boys quickly ran to one of these. They were safe as the train went past them. "That was too close! We could have died!" the boys told each other. "How do we always get ourselves into trouble?"

Sometimes as Voula rode along the country roads in the sunshine, she would look far away and she thought she saw water across the road. Bob told her it was a *mirage*! As they got closer to the "water", it disappeared. Then another watery pond looked like it was there, across the road far away.

Those long, summery days seemed to last a long time, because the children did a lot in one day! They wished their games would never end, as each one loved being together with the other kids and sharing the beauty around them. With every colourful sunset, they had to go home for dinner. They said goodbye to their friends with a bit of sadness, that such a great day of fun had ended, and it would soon be time to go to bed! (1357 words)

left: a mirage on the road

right: a timber railway bridge

Voula watches Peter riding his beloved bicycle and wishes she could do it too.

riding together at last!

Chapter 26
The Bicycle Lesson

Voula became very confident riding her bike. Now she felt she could teach Steven Hadis how to ride his bike too! (Actually it was his sister, Peggy's bike, but Peggy let him ride it because he didn't have one of his own.) The other boys Steven played with thought that he was a bit of a *chicken*, since he didn't mind telling them when he was scared. You see, Steven was very sensible and wouldn't do something he felt unable to do. Recently, Steven was feeling ashamed that he couldn't ride a bike, as even his sister, Peggy could ride one! Anyhow, when all the kids wanted to go for a picnic, or go exploring on their bikes, Steven had to be carried on someone's bike or just run along, so it made things a bit difficult. Therefore, finally one day, he told Voula that he wanted to learn to ride, like the rest of them. She immediately wanted to help him as she felt sorry for him, and also he was nearly two years younger than she, so she felt *motherly* towards Steven!

First she instructed him to sit on the bike seat and try to balance himself. Then, while she held the bike, it rolled down the gentle slope on the side of her house while Steven steered. He wobbled the bike a lot, but Voula was very patient with him and kept helping him. Steven said he was *hopeless*, which made Voula try even more to help him! So she kept telling him that he could do it if he didn't give up. They kept rolling down the little hill and walking up to start again. Up, down, up down. At last Steven decided he could do it! He was certainly starting to enjoy himself! He could ride a bike! Steven thanked Voula again and again, telling her that if she had not helped him he would never have been able to ride! Steven was really quite a humble little boy ...well not that little, because he was a bit chubby. Voula's heart grew with pride!

Since they were doing so well, (on a roll) Voula wanted to continue helping Steve, although Steven felt he had done enough for one day. He said he was feeling tired. However, Voula decided that Steven must try to ride down Billy Goat Hill. She told him, "If you can do this, you can ride anywhere. There will be no need for *any* more training. You can do it, I'm sure!" And looking into her happy eyes, he believed her.

They eagerly pushed the bike out of the front gate and over to the left side of the Hill, since they knew the road rules. Sadly, Steven's courage disappeared like fog on a sunny day, as he stood at the top of the Billy Goat Hill and looked down the road. "I can't do this! It's too hard; maybe another day." Steven's voice sounded scared, but secretly he wanted Voula to push him, so that if he failed, he could blame Voula for being too bossy. Luckily for Steven, Voula felt Steven would certainly succeed. "No, no you'll be okay. Trust me!" she begged. Her words made Steven feel brave and he decided she must be right. He got himself ready. "I'll do it," he told a happy Voula. She said, "I'll hold onto the back of your seat so you don't fall. Don't worry."

This was an important time. It was good that Peter, Jimmy and the other Hadis children were coming up the Hill, when they saw Steven ready to do what he had never done before! "What a moment!" thought Voula, "Steven will be so happy!" She could see it all in her mind: Steven riding along, laughing with the other boys as they went riding into the countryside, exploring new places. It would be great and she would get some credit for helping Steve to ride! She felt proud of herself and her heart nearly broke with joy for Steven. But of course, pride often comes before a fall!

"Go Steve!" Voula told him, holding onto his seat. However, Steve had changed his mind! "No. I'll fall. I…I'm not ready for Billy Goat Hill yet!" said poor Steve. Voula wouldn't give up. She was stubborn and told Steve about his near success. Steven pushed off with his legs and got his balance on the bike, as Voula held onto his bike seat. He rolled down the slope quite nicely and the other kids started cheering him.

About one-third of the way down the Hill, Steven picked up speed and Voula couldn't hold onto the seat anymore, because she couldn't run fast enough. So now Steven was on his own riding the bike. Fear was in his eyes! If it wasn't for the gravel on the side of the road, Steve might have made it all the way down Billy Goat Hill. Now, when he got on the loose gravel, he didn't have a chance. The gravel made him lose control of the bike. He got a bit off balance, which scared him and made him wobble. The bike seemed to have a mind of its own! Voula saw it all happening very slowly, like in a dream. The bicycle wobbled so much that Steven lost control of it. Steven only got about two-thirds of the way down the Hill, when he let out a scream of terror, but no one could save him. He fell hard and Voula held her breath. No one wore bicycle helmets in the 1960s, so Voula thought Steve might have broken his teeth or his arm or his neck!

Steven got up shakily on his feet as Voula ran to help him. He had fallen on his face, hands and legs which were scratched and bleeding. There were some stones under his skin. "Get away from me. This is all your fault!" screamed Steven. Voula was also hurt and upset by Steve's accident. They had spent a lovely, friendly afternoon together, as she helped him to learn to ride, and now this was her *thanks*. "I should not have told him he could ride down the Hill, and then everything would have been fine," Voula told herself sadly. "I've stuffed-up again!" It seemed she couldn't do anything right.

dinking or double-dinking was always popular

[circa 1935, Museum Victoria]

All the kids agreed with poor Steven that it was clearly all Voula's fault. Even Peggy, her closest friend was upset with her! Peggy told Voula she had been too bossy with her younger brother, so she didn't talk to Voula or play with her, for quite some time! (1105 words)

Chapter 27
The Childhood Home

What was Voula's, Peter's and Jimmy's house like? There is an old Australian dream or tradition, that every family can own their own home, with plenty of room for a *Hills Hoist* clothesline, on their own quarter acre block: about 1000 m² of land. This was true in Hamilton and I think it's still the case even today, like the expression, "A man's home is his castle". Nowadays of course, most people in Melbourne and Sydney live on land of about 650m² or smaller. Our politicians are telling us to reduce our dreams and not to be selfish by buying big blocks of land as it is increasing the sizes of our cities. An old Prime Minister, Paul Keating, said we should build upwards in Australia. Still, in country areas like Hamilton, people don't have the problems of big cities.

Voula's house in Byron Street was an old three-bedroom, weatherboard house, with a red, tin roof. It was then about sixty years old. The plaster on the walls was brittle and was cracking in places. Each room was painted a different pale colour: the boys' bedroom was blue and Voula's was pink. In the kitchen were two big storage containers, which pulled out at the top, from their base. They were built to hold grain, so they looked like big storage bins. Argyro kept her flour in one and her lentils

the kitchen with its pivoting storage bins, bottom left

horses pulling a cart

a Hills Hoist

a milkman with his crate of bottles

the "milko's" horse cart with milk cans

in the other. These types of storage bins are usually only found on outback properties and in the kitchens of places like Werribee House, as people of a hundred years ago couldn't get fresh food every day like we do these days.

When Argyro and Theo first rented a house in Hamilton, the refrigerators had no freezer, so ice was delivered every day and put in big metal boxes to keep meat frozen. Milk and bread were also delivered daily and money was left on the front porch for the delivery man. No one stole the money. And if the milk-man saw the milk bottles did not have any money in them, he knew the household did not want any milk that day. He checked the next day if there was any money left out for milk. If you were leaving for a holiday, you left a note for the *milko* in an empty bottle, telling him when you would return and want fresh milk. The milkman had a horse and cart with big milk containers and smaller milk bottles, in basket crates. He would run to each front door with a crate of bottles, collect the money, pick up the empty bottles and leave the correct number of full bottles. Bottles were made of glass and the milk came only in full-cream: not low-fat or calcium enriched. Then he would run to the next house as the horse slowly walked along the road without stopping. The *milko* and his horse were a great team and worked well together!

The house itself sat in the middle of the block, towards the front boundary, so there was lots of room on both sides of the house. As you stood facing the front of the house, there was a veranda with a camellia tree on the left side of the front yard. There was a huge palm tree

the palm tree from the back of the house before it was sawn down

on the right side of the garden that shaded the parents' bedroom.

After much discussion Theo and Argyro reached a decision to cut down the palm tree, because it made their room too dark and Argyro wanted more sunshine in their garden for their flowers. When a truck arrived, the children were ordered inside out of the way and out of danger. They watched from their parents' bedroom as some men unloaded a large circular saw. As the saw bit into the trunk of the palm tree, it made a loud screaming noise. The kids covered their ears but it did not help. They could still hear all the noise! Finally the palm came down, but it was so tall it fell on the camellia tree and broke some of its branches off. Argyro cried when she saw the broken branches with their beautiful pale, pink flowers, lying on the ground. When Theo tried to lift some of the branches he felt a sudden, sharp pain in his back. This back injury was to trouble him for the rest of his life. After that, Theo always gave advice to his children to take care of their backs. He said when one's back was hurt it was like glass with a crack in it: weak and never strong again.

In the garden, all around the fences, Argyro had planted flowers, mainly roses. Also, there was a curved, cracked concrete path going from the front wire gate to the veranda. That was where Voula tried to learn to roller skate. The four-wheeled skates had to be tied onto her shoes. They never really fitted properly, so it was difficult to learn how to skate. She could stand on her toes and go forwards on one leg but the cracks in the path made it hard to balance, especially on one leg. She never learnt

to skate backwards though, no matter how she tried and she always preferred her right leg to steady herself while the left was always raised. Why didn't Hamilton have a roller-skating rink like the ones she saw on the telly? She loved the graceful ice-skaters! Their smooth movements made poor Voula day-dream of becoming a famous figure skater one day, while her brothers wanted to be footballers and play for Essendon, their favourite team!
(933 words)

17 Byron Street, Hamilton, Victoria is an Edwardian style house built between 1900 and 1915. The pruned tree in front of the window on the left is still the same pink camellia tree of the 1960s! [2014]

a pink camellia flower

Nowadays the path has been repaired but it still leads to the same front gate.

tie on skates that were worn with shoes

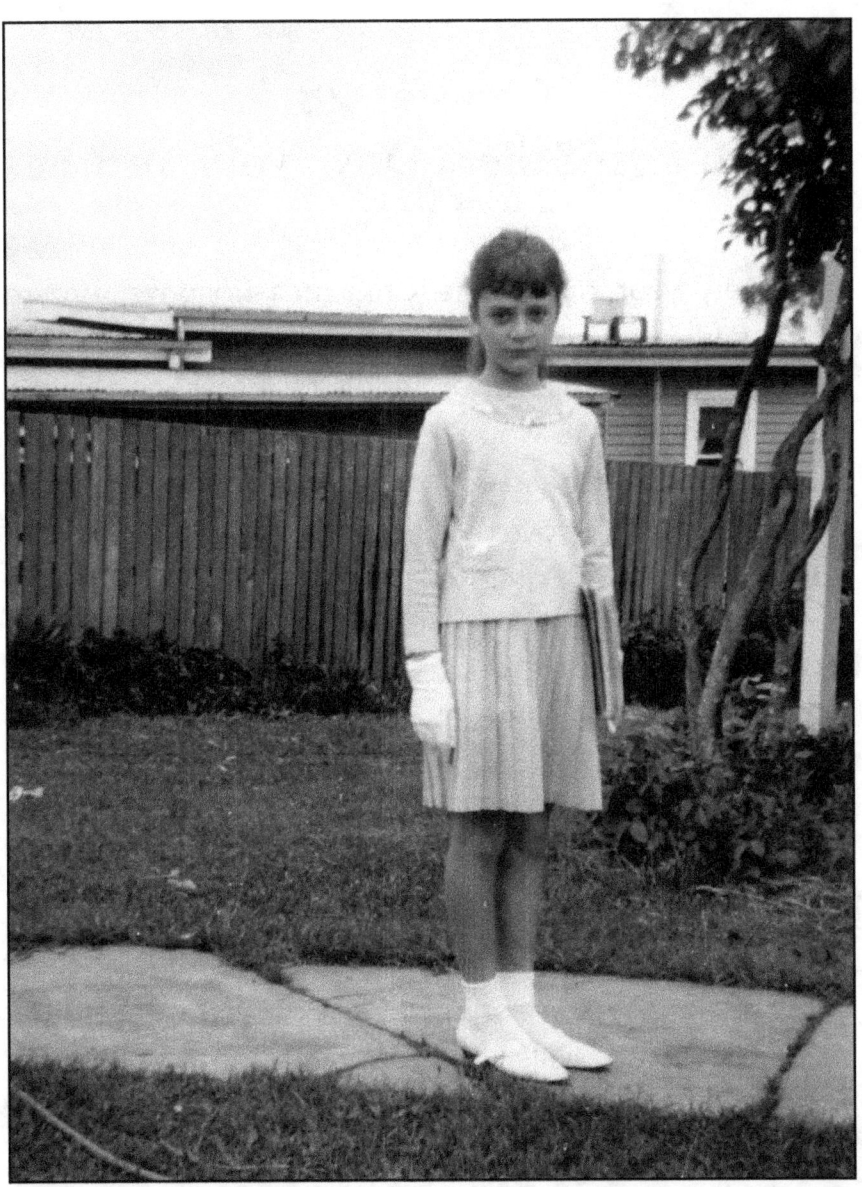

Voula is standing on the cracked path she practised her skating on. In the background is what remained of the camellia tree after it was hit by the falling palm tree.

Chapter 28
The First School Day Every Year

Every year during the Christmas holidays, Argyro would buy fabric from *Millers*. That store had all the different school uniform materials of the schools round about and mothers would come in, buy a few yards of fabric, and make their sons' and daughters' summer and winter uniforms. Argyro used her sewing skills to make Voula's new school dresses and the boys' shorts. At the start of every year, Voula went to school in a bright, new dress and Peter and Jimmy wore their new shorts. In those days, women had to sew their own kids' clothes or ask someone else to sew them. The Mothers' Club, at the school, also had people who could sew uniforms for a cheap price, if any mothers couldn't sew. Yes you could buy some uniforms from the store, as we do nowadays, but it was quite expensive and if you wanted a good fit you had to pay someone and get your clothes made. Argyro's sewing skills were appreciated by the Hadis family too. Every year, Mrs. Hadis bought fabric and gave it to Argyro to sew new dresses for Peggy.

It was always exciting starting the new school year: the children felt excited to be in a higher class level. Before the end of the year they had visited their new teacher in his or her classroom, to become used to them. The children were always excited and eager to visit their new teacher and felt they had grown up a little bit more. It felt good to think of the future and not to hang on to the past, which felt safe.

When Voula started grade five, Miss Slater handed out exercise books for the different subjects. The children carefully wrote their names on the front of each book and put them into their desks. Then they took them home for their mothers to cover them with brown paper, to protect them from damage, as the exercise books had to last a whole year!

Two pupils could sit at the double desks which had

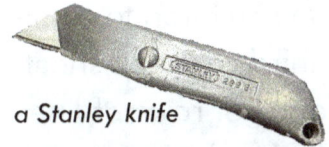
a Stanley knife

sheets of coloured paper and woven paper below

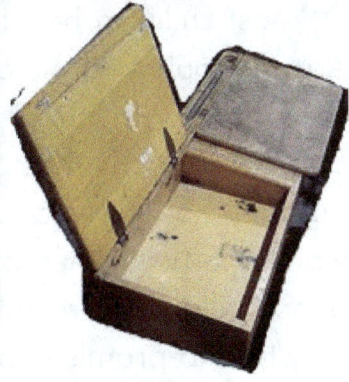

Jimmy and Voula are in their school uniforms on their way to school.

a double desk

lift-up lids, so they kept all their books, rulers and writing materials in their desks. For special art and craft lessons, the teacher would sometimes give out coloured squares of paper. It smelt fresh and the kids loved to smell the new paper. One day Miss Slater gave out *three* pieces of fresh, coloured squares, with strict instructions not to do anything with it until she told them. It was expensive and not to be wasted by mistakes. She showed them how to use their rulers and pencils to draw measured lines on two of the coloured squares of paper. Then she gave out scissors and showed the class how to cut along the lines to make long strips. Next she asked the children to come to her desk, one at a time, with their third coloured sheet. At her desk she used a Stanley knife to cut rows of lines on their paper. Finally she showed the class how to weave a pattern onto the paper she had cut, by using the strips. There were many different patterns and Miss Slater used the woven paper to teach about the art of weaving, and to teach words like *waft* and *warp*. Hamilton was the *wool capital of Australia*, so weaving and wool spinning were interesting facts for the children to learn.

Most children had their own set of coloured pencils. Argyro would shave the ends of the pencils and write her kids' names on them. Coloured sets of *Faber Castel* or *Derwent* were the most popular. *Derwents* were expensive but they had silver and gold colours, which all the kids wanted to use! When pupils were colouring-in, these two pencil colours were often borrowed by classmates, but they had to promise not to use up the pencils too much! So anyone who owned *Derwents* was popular during

a coloured pencil set

a wooden pencil case with a slide off lid

a nib pen needed to be dipped in ink

Voula's name is on a red pencil

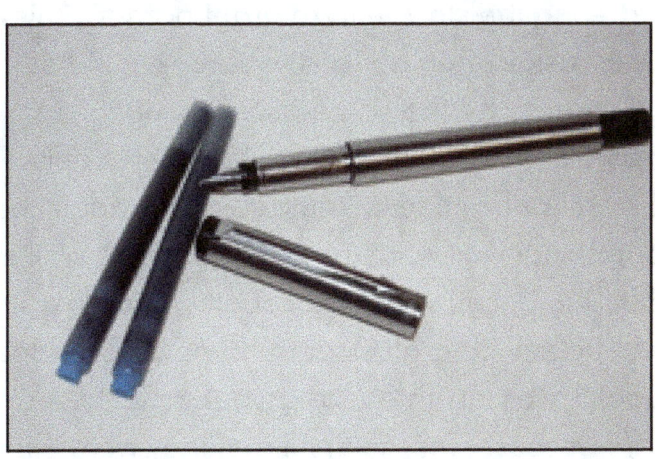

a fountain pen with its ink cartridges

colouring-in and craft lessons. Voula discovered a secret way of making her colours brighter and deeper: she used to put water on the tips of the pencils and she kept the secret to herself! But, before the end of the year, she told the other kids.

Grade 5 was also the year pupils went from using an ink nib to getting a *fountain pen licence*, but only if their teacher thought that their ink nib handwriting was *up to scratch*.

Blotting paper and ink were needed for good nib writing and the pupils had to take good care not to make a mess when they were writing. Normal ball-point pens were not allowed to be used by pupils until the middle of grade 6. That's because teachers thought children's writing would *go to pot* if it wasn't carefully practised with a nib and lots of concentration.

Social Studies, in grade 5, were all about the Australian explorers, like Burke and Wills. They also studied the cultures of other countries. Because Voula was one of the few children in the class with migrant parents, Miss Slater sometimes asked her about the Greek culture. Kids at that age want to be the same as other kids, so Voula felt embarrassed when Miss Slater asked her to tell the class what she ate for breakfast. Voula said "porridge" because she thought that was what the other kids ate. Well it was a little white lie, because Argyro usually made her children toast and eggs with a glass of milk; never porridge!

Grade 5 was an interesting year and the pupils felt important because, for the first time, they were allowed to use compasses, and stencils of Australia and Victoria, to trace maps into their exercise books for geography. These were bought from newsagents. There were little holes in the stencils for the capital cities, and for the borders of the states, so you could use a sharp pencil to make dots there.

Another thing that they learned in grade 5 was to have turns taking *weather readings*. Each day, outside in the school ground, they measured the air pressure and temperature from a barometer, and the rain level using a water gauge.

That year, to get some money for charity, Miss Slater entered the beauty contest in the Hamilton Show. She blushed when the headmaster, Mr. Harris, announced during school assembly that she was the winner. Seeing her, the kids realised that teachers might feel shy too. She quietly explained to them that she had wanted to help make some money for charity, and not that she felt herself to be beautiful! Anyhow, the class was proud of her because she was such a caring and interesting teacher. They felt that the other grade 5 teacher was not as good as their teacher!
(1119 words)

A school colouring book about different cultures: this one has Greece in it.

Here is Voula's writing using an ink nib. You can also see the deep red on the bottom right, because she used water on the pencil tip.

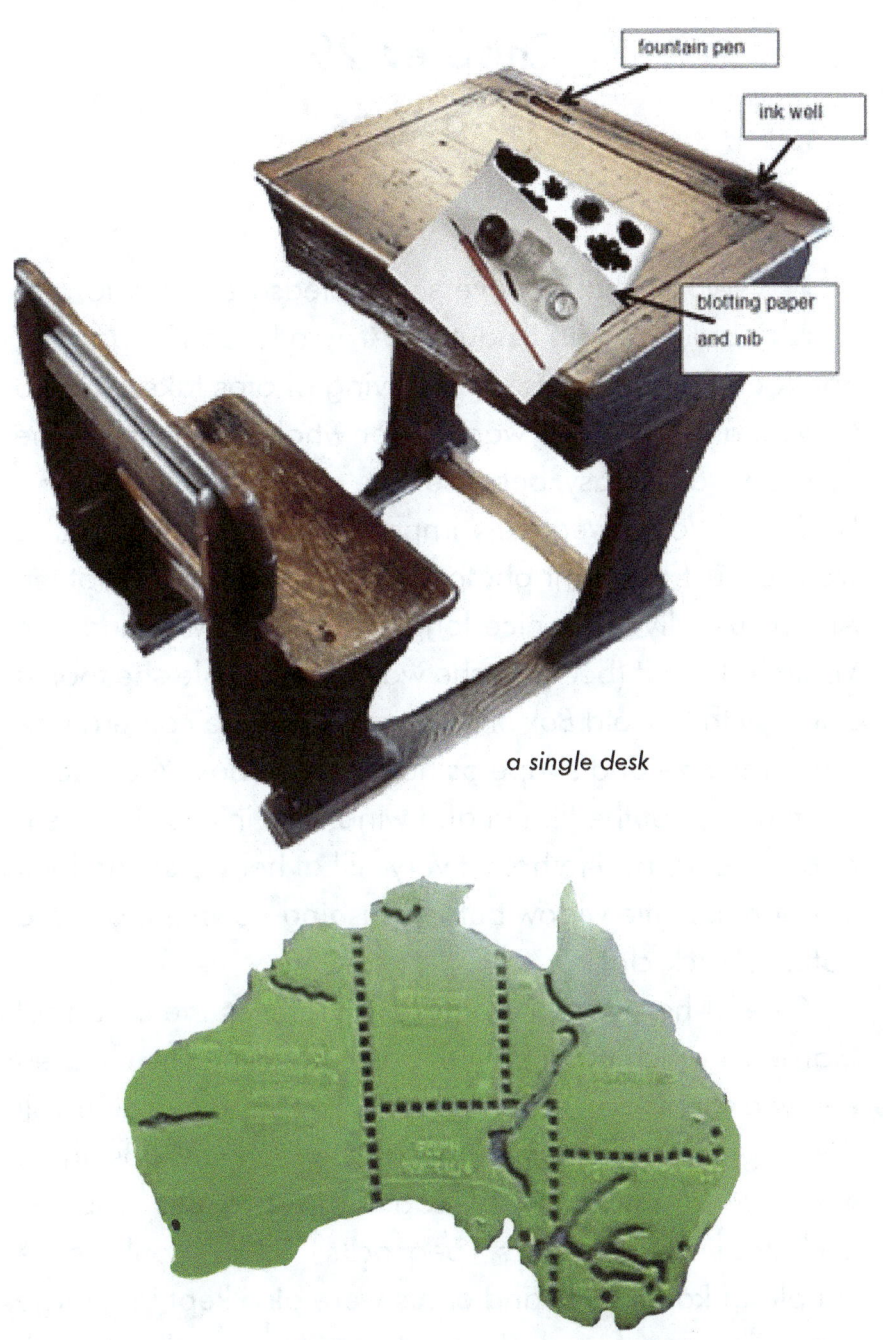

a single desk

a stencil of Australia

Chapter 29
Pleasures

Everyone should have some pleasure in life to give it balance with its duties. Argyro loved her garden. She took a lot of pleasure in having photos taken next to flowers and she often wanted her whole family to do the same. It wasn't easy, because, like many children, Jimmy, Peter and Voula were very impatient and did not want to wait for just the right photo to be taken by their mother. Argyro usually cut a nice long-stemmed flower and told Voula to hold it (because she was a girl), while she took a photo with her old *Box Brownie* camera. The camera was the same size and shape as half a tissue box. You had to open it up, put the film in and wind it up inside. To take a photo Argyro had to hold it very still at her waist and look through the little widow before pushing down the camera button, "click-clack".

One of her favourite places to visit was the Botanical Gardens, which had many beautiful flowers. The children enjoyed the space of the Gardens where they could roll down grassy hills and play. In the early 1960s there was also a small zoo of caged guinea pigs, rabbits, cockatoos, budgerigars, peacocks and monkeys. A couple of kangaroos and emus were also kept in a large area. There was a duck pond you could walk around,

Argyro, in her eighties, is posing in front of some beautiful roses, in full bloom.

Voula hated her hat!

With their aunt and cousins, at her house in Preston.

the Box Brownie and its negative

with an island in the middle. Near the cages were some swings and a see-saw too, and near the tall fountain was an old canon you could sit on.

One day the family travelled from Hamilton to Melbourne for a holiday. At Argyro's sister's house, Argyro wanted a photo of their time there. It also gave Argyro the chance to dress-up her daughter in a hat. She put it on Voula's head and then, as usual, gave her a flower to hold for the photo. It was a lily. Argyro's sister waited to take the photo, but Voula wasn't happy at all. She didn't want to take the flower from her mother! And she hated wearing her hat! However, Argyro thought it would look nice to have a photo with flowers in the background, and she ordered her daughter to hold the lily and to smile. She was very upset that her one and only daughter did not want to obey her! Argyro could not persuade Voula. She just couldn't understand why Voula was such a stubborn girl! Flowers fade quickly, and both Voula and the lily drooped!

Argyro also wanted to take photos of her family in flower beds, even though the kids thought it was silly. They hated waiting and waiting and waiting, while their mother took her time for just the right photo. Of course Argyro wanted to take snap shots to remember what life was like for her family, but her kids couldn't care less!

Even in her nineties Argyro kept vases of flowers on her kitchen table, and she loved her roses. Her favourite ones were those with a perfume, especially the red roses. No one seemed to have hay fever in the 1960s or maybe they didn't know much about it back then. Argyro would

Here is a sample of Argyro's outdoor photos, with [of course] flowers in the background. Jimmy is in his school uniform. Argyro in her nineties.

cut lots of flowers and put them in vases all over her house.

Since their house had land all around it, Argyro had lots of space to grow flowers, as well as to make a big vegetable patch in her back yard. She grew tomatoes, spinach, pumpkin, beans, potatoes and silverbeet too. There was lots of parsley, mint, oregano and basil too.

As the front and back yards were easily reached, it came in handy, when Deidre visited. This girl was in Peter's grade, but she was also Voula's friend. Argyro allowed Deidre to bring her pet horse over when she visited! The kids could all take turns riding it around and around the house, until Deidre thought it was time to go home.

There was another very good thing about Deidre: her parents owned the local milk bar. Anyway, Deidre was a kind girl and often had a bag of lollies to share with her friends. Peter's favourites were bubble-gums because he liked the footie cards that came with them. Voula's favourites were milk-bottles and raspberries. They are still around. Jimmy liked all lollies—he had a sweet tooth. It may interest you to know that Jimmy grew up to become a dentist and he advises his siblings not to eat sweets! Life is funny isn't it? By the way, Voula's and Jimmy's favourite drink was *Fanta* and Peter's was *Pepsi*. Tasty soft drinks were made by the *Tarax* Company, and were delivered in glass bottles in a crate, to the house. They used to have bottle caps on them and some people liked to collect all the different kinds of caps, as a hobby. Sadly, *Tarax* has gone out of business.

Did you get pleasure from climbing trees in your

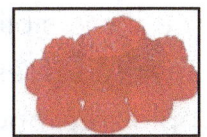

raspberry and milk-bottle lollies

a Tarax bottle and bottle cap

Deidre is on her horse and below is her parents' Milk Bar in 2014.

Peter is up highest on the apple tree and Peter G is on a lower branch. Jimmy and Voula preferred their feet on the ground! The garage and woodshed are behind them.

the apple tree today

childhood? The three siblings, from a young age, loved climbing all the fruit trees in the back yard. There was a smallish apple tree and several different plum trees. The apple tree had a horizontal branch that they thought looked like a horse, so they tied a rope to it and bounced on the branch, pretending to ride it like a horse. That was fun until it broke under their weight, and their mother was upset that it would not bear many apples.

Argyro told her children they should take better care of their trees, so they would get fruit from them. They decided that each of them would look after a tree and soon chose which trees belonged to whom. Peter wanted the tallest plum tree, near the back fence, from which he had hung the "monorail". It had small yellow plums. Jimmy wanted the thick tree with the biggest and reddest plums, as he found it easiest to climb and have as his own. This was the tree to which they tied Voula when she was the Indian in their game of *Cowboys and Indians.* When Argyro came to the back door and called them in for lunch, the boys left her tied to the tree!

Voula had the plum tree with the medium-sized, red plums next to the swing, along the side fence. This tree had a branch growing almost horizontally across its trunk, at about two and a half metres from the ground. She could climb onto the cross-bar of the swing, get onto the top horizontal beam of the paling fence, and then onto the tree. However it was very uncomfortable because both of her shoes couldn't fit in the small angle of the branches. It was hard to stand sideways on one shoe and admire the views of the neighbours' gardens.

Voula decided she needed to get more comfortable and build a tree-house in her plum tree, but couldn't do it by herself. Argyro was very handy and nailed a plank of timber on the tree, making a wonderful platform for Voula to stand on with *both* feet! The horizontal branch made a natural fence for her to lean on, which she held onto tightly, because she was afraid of heights. Voula was very happy! This was *her* tree house and it gave a great deal of pleasure! She was often seen climbing carefully onto her tree-house at dusk, so she could watch the sun go down on the horizon. The colours of the sky were amazing and she loved the hills and trees she could see everywhere! She came to think of nature as her personal friend. Whenever she felt lonely, Voula climbed onto her tree house and was comforted.

For her twelfth birthday the oldest Hadis kid, Theo, gave her a gift of a few crystal gems he had bought and also some that he had dug up. Theo enjoyed looking for gemstones as a hobby with his friend and neighbour, a boy of about the same age. Theo attended *Hamilton College*, one of the best private schools in Hamilton. All the other kids thought he was serious and like a grown-up, because he was usually in his bedroom studying. Theo Hadis grew up to become a lawyer and run his own business, so his hard work paid off. Voula took the crystals up to her tree-house to admire them in the golden, glowing light of the setting sun. She saw the sparkling light and colour of her gems. Voula wanted to keep them on her tree where she could enjoy them alone, at her favourite time of the day. Taking a rusty knife from the garage, she cut out some little holes in the branches of her tree-house and carefully placed a crystal into each of them. There they remained for her pleasure and secret delight, shining as the sun hit them.

Every evening, just before dusk, it became a celebration to climb her tree, see what was happening in the neighbouring yards and then look towards the hills on the horizon. Have you noticed there is a special kind of golden light at dusk? During those few minutes of golden sunlight, when the light shone on her gems, Voula would look at the colours of each crystal and admire their beauty. They were all of different sizes and colours, so they all sparkled differently. Voula pretended she was a princess and felt richer than a king in her tree-house! In the end though, Voula did *not* keep her crystals, but more of that later.

Another pleasant thing about Hamilton was a celebration called *Yulunga*, an Aboriginal word meaning "dance". Crowds would gather along Gray Street and outside Lucas Café to watch the *Yulunga Parade*. There were clowns, people on stilts, jugglers, decorated floats and music bands marching by. It was fun, colourful and interesting. Everyone helped; even the kids who would decorate their bikes and ride them in the parade. One year Peter and Bob put streamers through the spokes of their bikes. Their bikes looked wonderful as they slowly rode them along in the parade. Jimmy and Voula cheered like mad for their brother, who had spent ages cleaning and decorating his beloved blue bike (with its bent bell). (1704 words)

Hamilton College became The Hamilton and Alexandra College in 2001.

the official Yulunga logo

Voula felt like a princess.

some crystals from the volcanic regions of Hamilton

a clown on stilts in a mid seventies parade

the King and Queen of Yulunga(?) on a decorated float

Chapter 30
The Club

Disneyland was built by Mr. Walt Disney in the mid- 1950s and it was an exciting new idea and very popular, because it got into people's imaginations. There was *Fantasy Land, Tomorrow Land* and *Adventure Land*. In the 1960s, on Saturday evenings at 6:30pm, on Channel 7, everyone watched *Walt Disney's Wonderful World of Colour*. It was never missed by anyone; it was very popular. Peter, Voula and Jimmy came running into the lounge room to watch the television when they heard the show's song, "When I wish upon a star".

They loved watching Disney movies and Mickey Mouse and his friends were popular too. There was even a Mickey Mouse Club in the United States! Watching Disney movies was the start of Voula's love of movies and watching some great adventures. The four Hadis kids, Voula and her two brothers sometimes watched together, but most of the time they didn't watch TV, because they were too busy doing things together. It was on Disneyland's *Tomorrow Land* that Peter first saw a monorail and he was very excited to see it! That is when he decided to build his own monorail, by using his broken billy-cart. They had hung it on the back plum tree as you read in Chapter 22.

One day, on TV, they saw something about the Scouts

Walt Disney is surrounded by famous Disney characters.

popular books for children at the time

for boys, Girl Guides for girls and Brownies (for little girls) and it made them wish they could be in a club like that too. Of course some of their school friends were boy scouts and girl brownies too, but Argyro and Theo were not comfortable about their kids joining Aussie clubs, because of the different culture. They didn't know it was begun by Christian churches to help children develop upright morals and experience the outdoors, especially those children who had lost fathers during WW2. Also in those days parents worked hard and many did not think activities outside school were very important at all, except maybe learning to play a musical instrument. They thought that clubs and sports were just something kids did to stay busy. Most parents thought it was just playtime. For these reasons, Voula's parents never went to any of her netball games on Saturday mornings, or to any of Peter's footy matches; some parents did, but most were working. Anyway, the seven children were together one day when Voula suggested how nice it would be to make their own club, and that's just what they did!

Everyone had to give 5 cents to become a member and the money would go into the club's piggy bank. After all, if they could save something today, they will have something tomorrow! After some talking they decided Jimmy and John were too young to have any money and that they could be members of the club for free. Here is a little history and explanation about the club.

1. Voula wanted to call it the "Peacock Club", but had to negotiate, because the boys didn't like Voula's bossy leadership and decided not to become members.

scouts in the 1970s

This type of book was popular in the 1960s and shows a happy girl in a club uniform, no doubt doing interesting things.

2. Voula realised the club would not even start, unless she had their support, so she told them it would be *their* club, asked Steven Hadis to be the president, and asked them for their ideas for the club's name.

3. They voted, and because there were more boys, they finally decided on the "PRINCE and PEACOCK CLUB". Prince was the family dog and they wanted his name for the club. Voula pushed to get the J for "justice" as she could see rules would be needed. She wanted the boys not to argue with her. To interest them and to show them that the club really was *theirs,* Voula wrote a *logo* using the letters: J for "justice", P for "Prince", and another P for "Peacock".

4. Still they weren't very interested until she told them the club, not *only* offered a *library of books* for members to borrow, but it could buy *lollies* for them and also *lend them money* from the piggy bank! Steven borrowed two cents straight away and one can understand why Voula introduced the *oath of loyalty*. She saw that his heart was a bit greedy for money rather than in the joy of being part of their club!

5. Rules included "no violence at meetings" due to the boys always arguing and fighting with her. Children can learn a lot about politics and diplomacy when they form a club!

Every club needs a constitution, so an exercise book was decorated by the Secretary, Voula, with some pink lolly foil and some silver chocolate foil, because it was shiny and she thought it looked classy. The words were a bit squashy though, as there was not much room, or

the original Peacock Club exercise book

planning of the layout. She did her best.

On the pink foil Voula wrote: "J.P.P CLUB
MONDAY 6th. 1. 69"

On the silver foil were the words: "PEACOCK JPP CLUB" and the club's logo followed by the secretary's initials,

to try to make the book look more official. Of course every good club has rules and an oath, and these were written on the silver foil:

"SILVER RULES

No Violence at Meetings" (Peter quite often liked to punch and fight!)

"Kindness and respect to elders" (Voula was the eldest!)
"OATH
We hereby swear to abide by the rules
and be forever loyal or pay the
consequences (No consequences were explained; just

the idea of them!)
MOTTO
LIVE & DIE KNOWN BY GOODNESS WITHOUT SLANDER"

(Sometimes the boys said nasty things about the girls.)

Before computers, the names of library books were kept in filing cabinets, in alphabetical order, on little cards. Also, each library book had a little cardboard pocket pasted inside its back cover, with the details of the book written on a slip of cardboard, kept inside that pocket. Voula busily stuck pockets and slips of paper into the back of each book that she and her brothers owned. She also made a pocket in the *Peacock JPP Club* exercise book for each member. The heading on the page is "Library Roll" in her fanciest writing. The library was now open for business. Late returns of books would probably be fined and the money would go into the piggy bank, *if* everyone co-operated and obeyed the rules, just like for real libraries.

The club was now begun and it was 6th January 1969! To make some more money for the *Peacock JPP Club*, the kids decided to knock on the doors of houses around the block, and ask if anyone needed any small jobs done for a small payment of 10 or 20 cents. It was a bit scary so

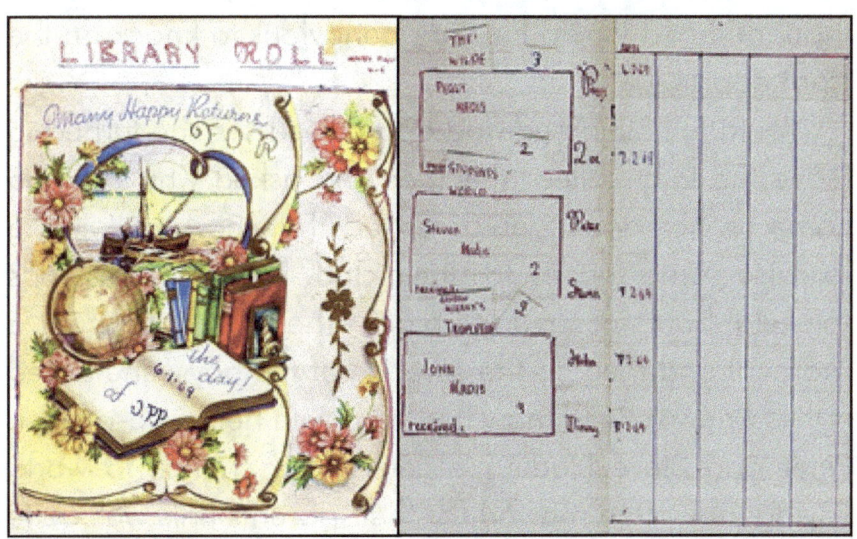

The Peacock Club started a library for its members.

The Club Book had pockets for each member. There is only one date entry as, unfortunately, books were only borrowed once before the library stopped!

they asked Argyro if she could come with them, but she said it would be better for the kids to go all together for safety, and that people would be kinder to kids rather than to adults. Well they knocked on quite a few doors, but either no one answered, or they didn't want anything done "at the moment".

At the last house, at the corner of the block, Voula knocked without much hope in her heart. She smiled politely at the serious-looking lady who answered the door. The lady wasn't interested in a bunch of hot-looking children who were in her front yard, and she frowned at Voula. "Why are you knocking on my front door? It's rude!" she spoke like an angry teacher. "You are not visitors, so the right thing to do, is to knock on my side or back door, like the trades people." Voula was shocked. She had heard of this sort of thing before, but had never thought that it would be rude behaviour to knock on the front door!

Voula felt ashamed and apologised. As she turned to leave the lady called after her and asked why she had come to her door. Voula replied that they were trying to raise some money for their club, by doing little jobs for neighbours around the block. The lady thought for a moment and then, to the surprise of the boys, she asked if they knew how to mow her lawn with her hand-mower. Peter and Steve Hadis jumped at the chance to work, saying they often mowed for their parents (this was quite true). The lady led them to the garage and they returned with her mower. It was hard work but the ground was level and she had promised the two boys 20 cents each!

While they were waiting, the girls and little boys did some weeding for free, to show they were good workers and nice kids. They wanted to build a good name with their customers! When they became tired they went home, but the boys were still mowing; taking turns. However, no one can remember what the club bought with the money the lady paid them. Probably it was chocolates and lollies, as they had agreed when the club started!

After this the children found it difficult to find more little jobs to do in the neighbourhood, so their money ran out. As happens in the real world, their business also died because they had no money to keep it going! Soon after that the children lost their interest in the club and they never did start any other club again! What a sad ending!

Now about the library: Voula tried to get back the books the kids had borrowed, when the library was first started. No one wanted to borrow any more books. After that, she just "borrowed" her own books and sometimes lent some to Peggy; that was all. Poor Voula felt a bit foolish and it had all been a lot of effort for nothing much. She felt it had been fun while it lasted, but also stressful trying to keep everyone interested. It was amazing that adults could keep their clubs going for years and years!

(1655 words)

a hand-pushed lawn mower

Chapter 31
The Sleepover

It was the end of 1968 and it was a sad and serious time for Voula, when she finished grade six at Gray Street State School. It had been her first and only school. She had attended it for most of her life, and it was where she came into contact with Aussies and their culture. For her, the school had been a cooking pot, boiling together the Australian, countryside culture of the 1960s, with the Greek culture of her parents. Voula remembered the happy times at primary school, of playing and being a part of girls' games, but she also realised she needed to make more of an effort to make friends with others kids. She thought about it for weeks and finally made herself a promise: she would try to make *lots* of friends, try to be accepted and popular. Somewhere she had heard: "If you want to have friends, then you have to be friendly". Yes! She would have a new start in high school, so she would try to fit in more. She wanted to feel accepted by Aussies and to not feel different from them, like an outsider! This was her serious promise to herself and something she would try hard to do. It was her New Year's Resolution! She told no one about her hope to become more popular with her classmates.

With the beginning of 1969, Argyro, as usual made Voula's new school dress, but bought the rest of her

Voula loved Hamilton High

"I shall attain" on the Hamilton High jacket pin.

In 1969 the siblings posed in their school uniforms, with the family pet, Prince. She is wearing her chain, the above badge on her jacket lapel and two different coloured pens are in her top pocket, ready for study! It was a school rule for long hair to be tied up.

uniform: a dark green, felt hat and a matching wool-blend jacket. The jacket and hat also had badges pinned on the front of them with the school motto: "I shall attain". When the time came to start Hamilton High, Voula was very excited. The teachers and buildings were unfamiliar and there were lots of them too. It took a lot of getting used to. She felt so grown up and noticed how the teachers treated the students with respect.

One of her most favourite classes was French. Because she was fluent in Greek, thanks to the determined efforts of Argyro, who insisted on giving her lessons, Voula found it easy to learn a third language. They do say that if you know a couple of languages, it is easier to learn a third and a fourth one. However, maybe it was the new method the French teacher used. This teacher decided to use the *audio-visual method*. This meant that students listened to an audio of French words while looking at pictures. They weren't allowed to read the words until the audio was repeated and pronounced correctly several times. After that, students were allowed to read what they had been practising how to say. The teacher thought this would help the students to have better pronunciation without trying to read the words. In any case, it worked well for Voula and she always got the highest marks for her tests, in the class.

Another favourite subject was science, because of the science laboratories. It was fun to use Bunsen Burners and tripods, Florence flasks, test tubes, clasps and cylinders. She learned a new style of writing too, that of *scientific experiments*. The exercise books were specially made for

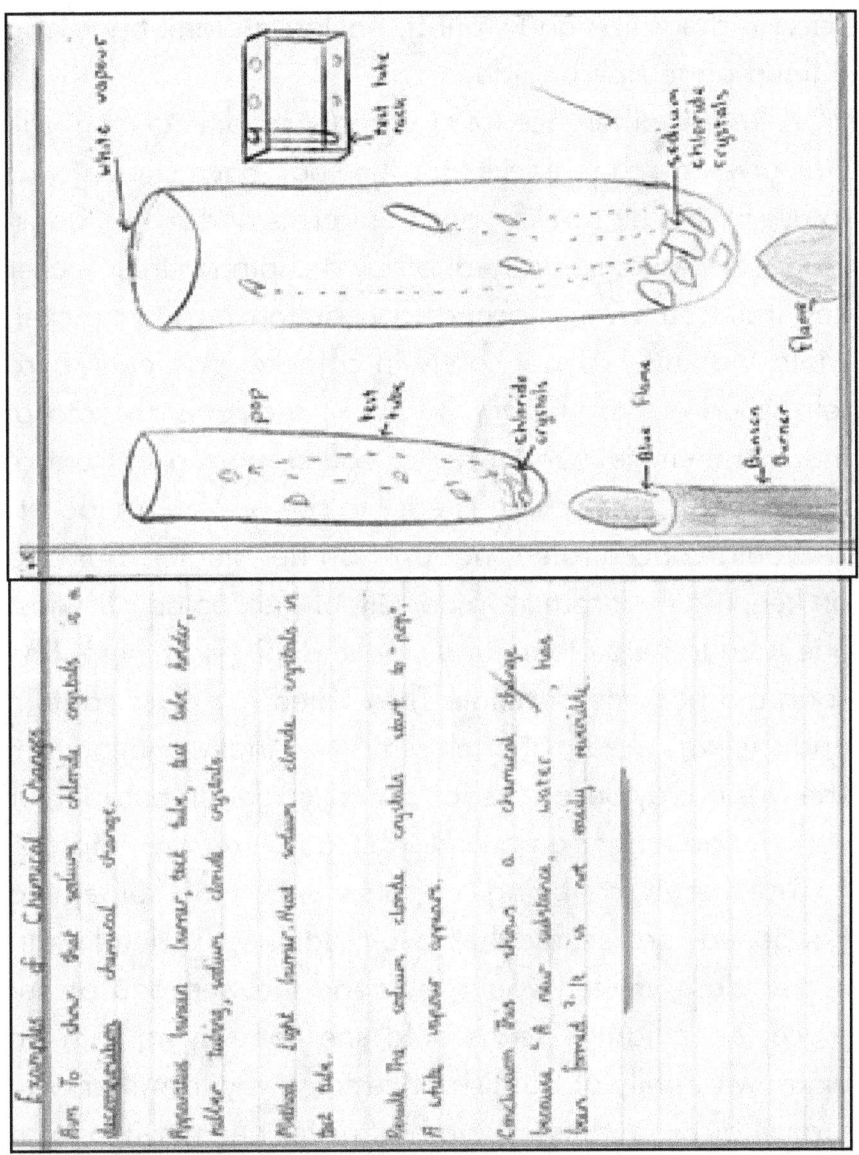

The exercise books for science had one ruled page for writing the experiments and one blank page for diagrams.

science diagrams and writing, having a blank page and a lined page side by side.

A further difference from primary school was that she was given a school locker for the year. Each student was to use it for their books, sports uniforms and school bags. Students were encouraged to buy a chain for their locker key that could be attached to a button on their jacket, while the key was put safely in a jacket pocket. Argyro felt proud of her "school children" and took a photo of them in their new uniforms; of course posing in front of her roses. The key chain is easy to see on Voula's jacket.

Voula concentrated, not only on her studies, but also on keeping the promise to herself, of making new friends. She tried to help others and say kind things to them. She soon did become popular! They voted her class captain and she was liked by her classmates. Finally, she thought she was happy because she was no longer an outsider, or was she no longer an outsider because she was happy?

The result of being popular was that something happened that scared her a bit. Janine, a friendly girl in her class, invited Voula to spend the weekend at her place, on a farm. How would she cope living with an unknown family of Scottish ancestry, away from her own family for two nights? Voula had never been invited for a sleepover before and she was not sure what her parents would say. It was something new for all of them.

After discussing it with Voula, Argyro and Theo made an unexpected decision: she could go to Janine's home for the weekend! So, after school on Friday, Janine's dad picked up Voula with Janine and drove to their farm. It was a large sheep farm with quite a lot of land. Everything seemed lovely, but the family was very quiet and Janine's parents ignored Voula after they welcomed her. To make things more uncomfortable, Voula found that she had to share a bed with Janine which was something she wasn't used to. To add to this, her friend was in the habit of not wearing underwear under her nightie! This seemed most strange to Voula and she lost her chattiness, becoming quiet and nervous. On Saturday the girls killed time walking around the farm and looking at the flocks and feeding the orphaned lambs, but Voula was homesick. Janine asked what was wrong but Voula only replied that everything was good.

After another uncomfortable and sleepless night, Voula tried to be outgoing and friendly, but with little success and felt relieved when she was finally driven home on Sunday afternoon. On Monday, at school, lining up outside a classroom and waiting for the teacher to arrive, the girls' eyes met. After saying hello Janine turned away and spoke to another girl. Janine wasn't very friendly anymore. She soon found a new best friend to be with. Well that suited Voula just fine! It would be easier not to talk to Janine. Still, it was a bad ending and Voula hoped she would still be popular at school. She worried that Janine would say negative things about her to the other students. One thing for sure: no more sleep-overs for her!

(1086 words)

Chapter 32
New Places

No one could believe it: a man was going to walk on the moon! It was Monday 21st July 1969, and Voula was going to classes at Hamilton High School. That day the principal of the school had told teachers to send groups of students to walk to nearby homes which had televisions. So at the beginning of lunchtime, Voula and some other students, from different class levels, walked to a schoolmate's house around the corner from the school, to watch the live telecast of Neil Armstrong taking his first steps on the moon!

Everyone was very excited to watch this historic event! But to tell you the truth, the black and white television was confusing because it was not clear. There was a lot of interference and static. Furthermore, even the speaking of the astronauts was not easy to understand. Anyway it was still a great time and everyone waited to watch it all happen. Then, at 12.56 Eastern Standard Time, Neil Armstrong stepped off the lunar module ladder and put his footprint in the moon dust. His now famous words were spoken, "That's one small step for [a] man, one giant leap for mankind".

Some people, including Theo, did not believe that it had really happened. For many years Theo's opinion was that it had all been a lie, so that the American scientists

the original facade of Hamilton High [now Brambridge College]

could keep on getting lots of money to spend on space travel. Yes, many people still think that the moon landing was all a *sham*. However, since that time much more information has been collected and there is little doubt that Apollo 11 really did land on the moon!

Some scientists thought that there would be a lot more moon dust on the surface of the moon, because the *Theory of Evolution* says that the moon is millions of years old. The moon dust made by meteors hitting the moon, stays on the moon's surface, because there is no wind to blow it away. So the moon dust was supposed to be very deep. However, Mr. Armstrong did not sink into the dust, but left a neat footprint a few centimetres deep. The moon must be much younger than millions of years old, so the *Theory of Evolution* is wrong about the age of the moon. Anyway, Neil Armstrong was a very brave man because they thought he might disappear into deep, deep dust with his first step!

At this time, there was a *Cold War* between the United Soviet Socialist Republic and the United States of America. The whole world was worried that either the president of the USSR or the president of the USA would "press the red button" to release a nuclear bomb. Everyone was afraid that if this happened, a nuclear war would mean the end of the world! Ever since 1962, and the problems in Cuba, the world was in trouble! There was an open contest between the Soviet Union and the USA, about which country would be the first to land and walk on the moon. Now of course, the USA was congratulating itself, but Armstrong, with his word of "mankind" joined

Armstrong's footprint on the moon's surface and their view of the Earth from the moon

the Lunar Module

The American crew of Apollo 11 were the first men on the moon. From left: Neil Armstrong, Michael Collins and Buzz Aldrin.

together all human hearts, from *every* country!

For the first time, we saw pictures of the Earth from the moon. Everyone understood how small yet very special our planet really is. Then, the popular school text book atlas, *Robinson's Primary World Atlas*, was replaced by the *Jacaranda Atlas*, because the *Jacaranda* had used some beautiful colour photos of the Earth taken from the moon. Everyone was amazed!

Voula too, along with her classmates, saw the Earth's beauty and how wonderful our planet is. "We must take good care of it," she thought. It was the topic of that time, because people started to seriously and publicly talk about looking after our planet. People thought about being *carers* of the Earth and of *protecting* it, for their children and grandchildren. Political groups were started, like *Greenpeace*, which formed in 1971. In Australia there was always a lot of rubbish thrown out of car windows onto our roads, so the government started the *Keep Australia Beautiful* advertising that same year.

During this time new groups were formed about pollution and keeping the planet clean and "green". Australia was the first country to have a "green" political party: the *Australian Greens* political party came out of the *United Tasmania Group* that was started by people who didn't want a dam on the Franklin River in 1972. Now, *The Greens* are part of Australian politics. Things were changing in Australia and in Hamilton too. Lucas Café was losing customers because the pubs were selling new "counter lunches". After sixteen years Lucas Café had to close its doors!

Theo and Argyro had been thinking about moving, as they were worried that their children would leave home one day to go to university. They wanted their kids to have a good education. Hamilton had excellent schools and many children went to boarding schools, for their secondary education, even to Geelong Grammar. Pete's best friend, Bob Tydon, boarded during the week and came home on weekends. When he got older, he left Hamilton to go to Melbourne University and study law. Theo was worried about the future for his children, for their education and that there were not many jobs in Hamilton. Where would their children find work? Therefore, like many families whose children were growing up, they "bit the bullet" and decided to move to the city–Melbourne.

Theo's and Andy's business partnership ended after fifteen years, when they told their landlord that they did not want to renew their lease for the cafe. No one bought Lucas Café from them; it simply closed its doors. After that, the Hadis family moved to Adelaide where Andy's wife had a brother and Theo took his family to Melbourne, where Argyro

the view from Billy Goat Hill with the two church spires

Australian Greens Party

Australian Greens website
Creative Commons

had a brother and two sisters. So many memories were left behind in Hamilton!

On the final morning, before they departed, Voula went out to look down Billy Goat Hill. Everything was sparkling and clean in the morning light. Even the power lines were decorated with dew drops that looked like diamonds, each perfectly round and beautiful. Voula stood and gazed at the view from the top of the Hill. She was trying to remember every detail. She didn't want to ever forget the pleasing view in front of her: there were the two church spires in the distance, surrounded by trees and houses. To her it was the most delightful view in the whole world. She was a romantic! Voula knew it was time to leave; it was time to grow up, but still the heart keeps a strong connection and love for home, the place of one's birth.

On the last evening before the family's departure, Voula climbed onto the single timber plank of her tree-house. For just one last time, she wanted to admire the view and her shining gemstones, sparkling in the golden light as the sun went down. Remember that she had cut holes into the branches of her tree-house and put her gemstones into them as decorations? Now she decided to leave them there, in the branches. They should stay where they belonged! Leaving behind her colourful gemstones was her way of showing her love for her special place.

When the family left for Melbourne it was September 1969. Voula felt her childhood was over. "I'll be back one day!" she promised herself. (In fact it would be about thirty years before she returned to Hamilton and be recognised by her old neighbour Don Shmitz, who remembered the

Voula's house in Hamilton as it was in 2014. As you can see not much has changed.

Voula in her tree-house, leaving behind her crystals

sound of her voice!)

Voula hated the idea of leaving Hamilton to live in the City! What would it be like? Her Mum told her there were a lot of Greeks, in Melbourne as it had the world's third largest Greek population in the world! It would be good to be with her relatives and some other Greeks. But the other thing she was worried about was becoming a teenager! She was a month away from her 13th birthday and Voula didn't like changes in her life. The move, and her thirteenth year of life, were both big ones! And how did her brothers feel? Peter didn't really want to leave his mate, Bob, but he was strong and didn't cry about it, and Jimmy didn't seem to mind too much.

Fortunately, Argyro and Theo were quite happy to have been able to buy a house across the road from Argyro's married sister, in Preston. Outside the house was a bus stop and the noise of the traffic continued day and night! What a change from the peaceful life they had known in Hamilton! Voula was too shy to roller blade on the footpath. All the passing traffic carried lots of people who would see her. Also, Argyro would not let her children ride their bikes. She thought the streets were too busy and dangerous for them. A year later, Prince, their pet dog, died on busy Bell Street. After getting out of the back yard through a hole in the fence, he chased another dog through the busy traffic and he was hit by a car! Argyro and Voula had run after him and saw it happen. They were heart-broken and Argyro wept on Voula's shoulder. They wished then that the family had stayed in Hamilton!

In any case, it was the end of their country life! A new

life in Melbourne had begun for the family. Jimmy's, Peter's and Voula's childhood home was left behind. Isn't that so for many of us? Isn't it true that life is like a book: with closing chapters and new beginnings? Perhaps *how* we live with other people is more important than *where* we live.

Finally dear reader, thank you for taking the time to share my childhood memories and to see life through my eyes. It has been difficult, at times, to share childhood experiences, with the mind of an adult. I have tried not to change the facts and the thoughts of Voula the girl, but sometimes her childish ways might have been influenced by my adult understanding.

Now, sadly, our journey together has come to a suitable end. Therefore, be well on *your* life's journey and let us say goodbye to each other with an old Irish prayer:

*Let us be thankful for life,
and for time's old memories
that are good and sweet.
And may the evening's light
find you gentle still.*

*May your day be touched
by God's blessings,
brightened by a song in your heart,
and warmed by the smiles
of the people you love.*

anonymous (1776 words)

Chapters for "Speak English Like Australians!"	Possible topical themes/issues for discussion	Literary Device	Example in text
1 Coming to Australia Proverb-we make mistakes, but by mistakes we can also learn. Slang-she'll be right mate, smoko	War, emigration, civil war, dowries, family duty, finding work, hope, responsibilities, tragic loss, cultural misunderstanding, racism, Australian culture, sexism, homophobia, violence	simile	He worked *like a dog*, to show the men he was working with, that he was not lazy.
2 Becoming an Aussie Proverb-good things always take time.	Assimilation, Cultural differences, language problems, loneliness, romance, dowries, marriage proposal, describing a person,	simile merisms hedging antithesis	chopping potatoes and grilling steaks like an expert -cooking and cleaning -cleaned up and locked up the shop His English was pretty good She loved Greece, yet she was the one in her family who must leave it!
3 The Marriage Proposal Proverb= delay is the thief of time Colloquialisms-too hard basket; idiom: *the ends of the earth*	studying; asking the father permission to marry his daughter; loneliness; career vs arranged marriage; family responsibility & duty; procrastination, saving face; little white lies, making do		Concern for her family made her leave her people and her country!

4 Family Proverb-accidents will happen Slang=busybodies	Olympic Games, John Landy, motherland; British culture; White Australia Policy; pregnancy; children, pressure to produce a son; desire for sons, family name; poultice;	synecdoche	In fact, there were soon more <u>mouths</u> to feed
5 School Proverb- we cannot hide from ourselves. Slang=blah, blah, blah; beanie Colloquialisms=head-start; flat-out; boss-around	School; bullying, peer pressure; shaving a girl's head; class reader "John and Betty"; gender roles; misunderstandings; embarrassment; taunting; New Australians; kinder	hedging	-Voula was able to understand <u>quite a bit of English</u>. -It <u>seems</u> that children can be very cruel to one another!
6 School Ceremonies & Rituals Proverb- Those who want to sing always find a song. Colloquialism= butterflies *in her tummy*	nursery rhymes; demographics; honouring the flag, national anthem "God Save the Queen", free milk bottles; General Assembly; fainting; Patriotic Declaration; school song; sports houses; Athletics Carnival and a Swimming Carnival; allergies	merism	-an <u>honour and a duty</u> to show respect to your country

Chapters for "Speak English Like Australians!"	Possible topical themes/issues for discussion	Literary Device	Example in text
7 Imperial Australia Proverb- Real beauty, that never fades, is a good character! Colloquialism=finger-licking good	Monarchy vs republic; Australia's PM; loyalty to the Queen; imperial & metric currency & measurements; hot cross buns; shopping hours; fast food stores	tautology simile	-They didn't wear hats <u>for protection against the hot sun</u> -she ate them, <u>piece by piece</u> -Hot Cross Buns were <u>as precious as gold</u>!
8 Anzac Day Proverb- a friend in need is a friend indeed Slang=diggers Acronym=ANZAC	WWs1 & 2, Anzac Day and Parade, returned soldiers & RSL; respect; monuments, Allied Forces; Remembrance Day	anaphora	"A time to be born, a time to die, ... a time for war and a time for peace."
9 Katie and The Beatles Proverb- if you ask no questions, you'll hear no lies Colloquialism=small talk	Pop culture and teenagers, TV; fear of Anglo-Saxon culture; childish ignorance; mop top hairstyles; The Beatles; lying	metalepsis	-a 14-year-old daughter, Katie, who was just crazy about *The Beatles* music band (relating craziness of mind to teens who are passionate about music groups/singers and actually seem to lose their minds)

10 Music Proverb- person's ideas are coloured by what they see Slang=sissies	Singing, playing an instrument, performing on stage and TV, emotional bullying, music, determination vs laziness, competitions, team work, record; billeting;	epigram	It seems that <u>being famous may bring quick glory, but it also brings shame too!</u>
11 The Accident Proverb= =sleep cannot help you're your soul is tired attacking someone else is the best way to defend yourself Slang= scared stiff	Older sibling responsibility, accidents happen, emotional pain, fear, blame	climax	<u>looking</u> at the new comic books, <u>smelling</u> the new pages and <u>deciding</u> which one to buy.
12 Celebrations Proverb-change is as good as a holiday Idiom- on top of the world	God, prayer, faith, School dress parade, cinema, family love, newspaper story, school fete; Mothers' Club; national costume; school games	understatement	It was <u>a bit of an honour to win</u>!
13 Fun, Games and Pets Slang=chooks Proverb-it is good for your soul to tell what you have done that is wrong	Fighting, injury, caring for pets, punishment, pain, embarrassment, fitting-in	hendiadys	She got <u>sick and tired</u>

Chapters for "Speak English Like Australians!"	Possible topical themes/issues for discussion	Literary Device	Example in text
14 At Home Proverb=a woman's work is never done slang=chooks	Girls and boys roles, housework, pocket money, training children; chores; fun, The Lone Ranger; Cowboys and Indians	hyperbole	there seemed to be millions of them everywhere
15 Obsessions and Hobbies Proverb-It does not matter how slowly you go, so long as you don't stop.	Superstition, OCD, good & bad luck, stamp collecting	pun	Horses are loyal, straight-forward and very stable animals
16 The Woodshed Proverb-Honesty was not always the best policy! Colloquialism=twenty-four seven	Hide and seek, obeying & disobeying parents, adventure and excitement in games,	assonance	She made it safer by quietly moving the wood around and she remained there for ages.
17 The Hamilton Show Proverb-it's not often you get something for nothing Blended word= Sheepvention	Merino sheep, Scottish dancing, farm animals, fairy floss, carnival rides, Samson the Strongman	epiphoras	It was for showing farming animals and for sharing farming ideas about their produce.

18 Going for Sunday Drives Proverbs- without advice plans fail, but with many advisers they succeed Slang-counter-lunches	European settlement in Vic, Portland, business problems, no seatbelts in cars, road litter, Keep Australia Beautiful campaign, cigarettes & smoking in cars, Wannon Falls and Grampians	oxymoron	going nowhere
19 Guy Fawkes Night Proverb- There is no point crying over spilt milk	Bonfires, Guy Fawkes, cracker night, fireworks, ants pets; Penny Bungers, sparklers	personification	Andy had a 1956 Holden he had named <u>Spiro.</u>
20 Pets Proverb- she should not fear failure, but rather fear not trying Idioms=out of the blue	Mother Cat, Ginger, Prince, budgies, tadpoles, pigeon club; fledglings; saving a pigeon's life	tricolon	<u>watching, training and learning about</u> these interesting creatures
21 The Billy-Cart Proverb- it's the foundation that stands the test of time colloquialism= it was a fair bet slang-save face	Boys and girls roles, building a billy, neighbourhood kids, driving on the road, Billy Goat Hill; saving face	allegory	Two boys refused the help of a girl, Voula. They told her, "No girls allowed!" and wouldn't let her have a turn riding the billy-cart. (This story could be an allegory about the suppression of females in a male-dominated world in general, and particularly in the sport of car-racing. Are there many famous women in car-racing? It is definitely a male-dominated sport!)

Chapters for "Speak English Like Australians!"	Possible topical themes/issues for discussion	Literary Device	Example in text
22 The Monorail Proverb= necessity is the mother of invention Slang= busted; chicken	Disneyland, initiative, invention, guinea pig; monorail; no sympathy; "Sticks and stones will break my bones, but names will never hurt me!"	metaphor	-Who could be <u>his guinea pig</u>? -She had always been a <u>chicken</u>.
23 Sticks and Stones Proverb= the best method of defence is offence!	Boys fighting, bullying, racism, kids behaving badly to an adult	anticlimax	-hit on their <u>heads, chests and legs</u> -decided to take his medication; <u>do a bit of housework and then relax watching some TV</u>
24 The Pipe Tunnel and Prince proverb= Danger creates caution slang=chicken idiom- a close shave	Dangerous escapades walking through water tunnel, Grange Burn River, teaching a dog to swim, the Dog Catcher	cataphora	-When <u>she</u> stretched out her hand Voula couldn"t see it! -<u>He</u> was frightened and maybe <u>Prince</u> thought the kids had tried to kill him!?

25 The Bike Proverbs: don't plan evil and do bad things to others because it'll all come back to bite you! it takes courage to try new things, but it takes wisdom to accept you *can't* do everything Colloquialism=get even	Learning to ride a bicycle, Biking, exploring, revenge, danger on wooden railway bridges, water mirages, sunsets, beauty, mushrooming, companions	boosting hedging (used for academic writing)	-He was <u>certainly</u> starting to enjoy himself! It was <u>clearly</u> all Voula's fault. -<u>It seemed</u> she couldn't do anything right.
26 The Bicycle Lesson Proverb-pride often comes before a fall Slang=chicken Colloquial= I've stuffed-up again!"; on a roll	Empathy, maternal instincts, encouraging another, knowing your limitations, trust, fear, fault and blame, pride comes before a fall; peer pressure; courage	pun climax simile	-Referring to the bicycle lesson=Since they were doing so well, (on a roll) like a wheel. -Steve might have broken <u>his teeth or his arm or his neck</u>! -disappeared like <u>f</u>og on a <u>s</u>unny day
27 The Childhood Home Proverb= A man's home is his castle Slang= "milko"	Hamilton, house description of weatherboard with iron roof, garden, cutting down of big tree, roller skating	alliteration	a <u>c</u>urvy, <u>c</u>racked <u>c</u>oncrete path

Chapters for "Speak English Like Australians!"	Possible topical themes/issues for discussion	Literary Device	Example in text
28 The First School Day Every Year Proverb- It felt good to think of the future and not to hang on to the past, which felt safe. Colloquialism= *up to scratch*; go to pot; a little white lie	School uniforms, sewing, new classes, teachers; desks; Mothers' Club; ink pens, weaving, peer pressure, lending pencils, weather readings, the PA system	euphemism pun	-buy off the rack (mass produced) …if their teacher thought that their ink nib handwriting was <u>up to scratch</u>. (because the nib scratches on paper) up to scratch=reaches the correct standard of skill or ability
29 Pleasures Proverb-flowers fade quickly	Box Brownie camera, photos, posing, horse riding, favourite trees, lollies and drinks, Indigenous Australians, Yulunga Parade, Botanical Gardens; tree house; nature; crystal gems	anadiplosis Onomatopoeia metaphor	-a celebration called <u>Yulunga.</u> <u>Yulunga</u> is an Aboriginal word meaning "dance". -the spokes of their <u>bikes.</u> Their <u>bikes</u> looked wonderful click-clack flowers fade quickly and both Voula and the lily drooped

30 The Club Proverb- save something today, they will have something tomorrow	Mickey Mouse, Disneyland, Scouts & Girl Guides started by Christian churches, netball, footy, cooperation, forming club rules and a library; leadership; motto & oath; group politics	irony	She smiled politely... never thought that it would be rude behaviour to knock on the front door!
31 The Sleepover Proverb= If you want to have friends, then you have to be friendly	Aussie culture, Friends, popularity, starting high school, science & French classes, sleepover at a farm	paradox	She was happy because she was no longer an outsider, or was she no longer an outsider because she was happy?
32 New Beginnings Proverb= life is like a book: with closing chapters and new beginnings Idiom=bit the bullet	Selling and moving house and cities, space travel, the moon, photos from the moon, The Greens; the environment; gemstones; your life's journey	Apostrophe anaphora	Finally, dear reader, thank you... Voula knew it was time to leave; it was time to grow up, but

How to use book discussions to write an essay

Here is a suggestion of one possible way to write an essay by referencing events from *Chapter 26 The Bicycle Lesson*.

Topic: "Peer pressure is a cause of drug abuse in teens. Discuss."

An essay plan could look something like this...

<u>Plan</u>

- introduction: don't trust friends making your own decisions
- paragraph 1: friends might mean well but lack experience
- paragraph 2: Voula pressures Steven– friends, drugs, danger, crime
- paragraph 3: peer-pressure; parents– time, watch for changes
- paragraph 4: parents– teach what to do
- paragraph 5: parents– praise; strong bond
- conclusion: good friends; drugs– health; say no; degradation

<u>Following the above plan, start your essay.</u>

Although friends may have good intentions when they advise each other, the outcomes can be far from helpful, and may cause pain and injury too, both to themselves and to those who love them.

When Voula patiently helped Steven to learn to ride a bicycle, her little life-experience resulted in her giving terrible advice to Steven. After hours of practising together, and with much encouragement from Voula, Steven really did improve his riding skills until he was able to ride unaided. However, due to Voula's lack of experience, she wrongly concluded Steven would be now able to ride down the steep local hill. Her positive attitude and certainty persuaded an equally trusting Steven, to trust her wrong judgement of his skills, much to his hurt, when he fell and injured both his body and his confidence!

In the same way, peer pressure is common and often misapplied, especially with teenagers looking for acceptance and friendship by taking drugs from friends. Encouragement to use drugs, from friends, who also have little experience of life, is dangerous and may lead to life-threatening addictions, bad health and painful relationships with family and relatives. The need for money to buy drugs will one day lead to crime and more and more violence that cannot be forgotten, due to their evil results. Perhaps even murder will be committed, while under the influence of drugs.

Parents must spend time with their teens, getting to know what is going on in their lives at school and if their friends are reliable or a negative influence. They must watch for any changes in behaviour and personality too as these may be warning signs.

Another responsibility of parents is to make strong children and teach them how to behave if a friend offers them drugs. They can also explain that they are "not into drugs" and walk away to find other friends to be with, or perhaps suggest playing a video game or watching a movie.

Also, parents need to build strong loving relationships with their teenagers and praise them every time they succeed, make a determined effort, face their fears, work hard or do an act of kindness. In this way children will more likely ask for help and advice from their parents, rather than trusting in the ideas of their friends.

Teenagers need friends, but they must be good ones and not bring disaster into the lives of children and their families too. Drugs can cause mental health problems that take a very long time to cure and sometimes never. Train teenagers to say no to drugs and explain the reasons very clearly to stop them taking well-meaning advice from "helpful" and "excellent" seeming friends. Parents must take responsibility to build strong bonds with their children and train teens to be street-smart and wise, by being strong, even with their often ignorant "besties" who may encourage drug use, which is only the start to a life of degradation, pain and shame for everyone around them!

(498 words)